Please remember that this is a library book,
and that it belongs only temporarily to each
person who uses it. Be considerate. Do
not write in this, or any, library book.

WITHDRAWN

D1609299

A S S E S S M E N T

S T A N D A R D S

FOR SCHOOL MATHEMATICS

167666
VC Lib

A S S E S S M E N T

S T A N D A R D S

FOR SCHOOL MATHEMATICS

Prepared by the Assessment Standards
Working Groups of the National Council of
Teachers of Mathematics

May 1995

NATIONAL COUNCIL OF
TEACHERS OF MATHEMATICS

Copyright © 1995 by
THE NATIONAL COUNCIL OF TEACHERS OF MATHEMATICS, INC.
1906 Association Drive, Reston, VA 20191-1593
All rights reserved

Second printing 1997

Library of Congress Cataloging-in-Publication Data:

Assessment standards for school mathematics / prepared by the
    assessment standards working groups of the National Council of
    Teachers of Mathematics.
        p.   cm.
      "May 1995."
      Includes bibliographical references.
      ISBN 0-87353-419-0 (pbk.)
        1. Mathematics—Study and teaching—United States—Evaluation.
      2. Curriculum evaluation.
      QA13.A878 1995
      510′.71′273—dc20   95-17267
                                                                     CIP

Permission to photocopy limited material from the *Assessment
Standards for School Mathematics* is granted for educational purposes.
Permission must be sought for commercial use of content from this
publication when the material is quoted in advertising, when portions
are used in other publications, or when charges for copies are made.
Use of material from the *Assessment Standards for School
Mathematics,* other than those cases described, should be brought
to the attention of the National Council of Teachers of Mathematics.

Unless otherwise noted, photographs are by Patricia Fisher.

Printed in the United States of America

The Assessment Standards Working Groups

Management Working Group

Thomas A. Romberg, *Project Director*	University of Wisconsin—Madison
Linda D. Wilson, *Assistant Director*	University of Delaware
Marvin E. Smith, *Research Assistant*	University of Wisconsin—Madison
James D. Gates, *ex officio*	National Council of Teachers of Mathematics
Mary M. Lindquist, *ex officio*	Columbus College, Georgia
Jack Price, *ex officio*	California State Polytechnic University
Norman L. Webb, *Consultant*	University of Wisconsin—Madison

Standards Working Group

Jeremy Kilpatrick, *Chair*	University of Georgia
James W. Wilson, *Assistant Chair*	University of Georgia
Diane J. Briars	Pittsburgh Public Schools, Pennsylvania
Jane D. Gawronski	Escondido Union High School District, California
Ed Reidy	Kentucky Department of Education
Maria Santos	San Francisco Public Schools, California
Denise Spangler Mewborn, *Research Assistant*	University of Georgia

Purposes Working Group

Jane D. Gawronski, *Cochair*	Escondido Union High School District, California
Diane J. Briars, *Cochair*	Pittsburgh Public Schools, Pennsylvania
Sandra P. Marshall, *Co–Assistant Chair*	San Diego State University/CRMSE, California
Mark Driscoll, *Co–Assistant Chair*	Education Development Center, Massachusetts
Harold Asturias	California Renaissance Project and New Standards Project
Ruth Cossey	Mills College, California
Clare Forseth	Marion Cross Schools, Vermont
Dennis L. Garvin	Baltimore County Public Schools, Maryland
Marieta Harris	Memphis City Schools, Tennessee
Jeane M. Joyner	North Carolina Department of Public Instruction
Susanne Lajoie	McGill University, Quebec
Diana V. Lambdin	Indiana University
Richard D. Lodholz	Parkway School District, Missouri
Mari Muri	Connecticut Department of Education

Outreach

Portia C. Elliott, *Coordinator*	University of Massachusetts at Amherst
Thomas Lewis	Moline School District, Illinois

Support Staff

Margaret H. Powell, *Editor*   University of Wisconsin—Madison
Kathleen Steele, *Production Editor*   University of Wisconsin—Madison

Resource Group

Sherry Beard   Bellevue School District, Washington
Alan J. Bishop   Monash University, Australia
Sharon R. Chavez   San Felipe Pueblo Elementary School, New Mexico
John A. Dossey   Illinois State University at Normal
Glenda Lappan   Michigan State University
Douglas McRae   Monterey, California
Rep. Annette N. Morgan   State of Missouri
Nel Noddings   Stanford University, California
Andrew C. Porter   University of Wisconsin—Madison
Edward Roeber   Council of Chief State School Officers, District of
                                Columbia
Ramsey W. Selden   Council of Chief State School Officers, District of
                                Columbia
Lee V. Stiff   North Carolina State University
Vance Wilson   University of Delaware
Dennie Palmer Wolf   Harvard University, Massachusetts

TABLE OF CONTENTS

ACKNOWLEDGMENTS

For more than fifteen years the National Council of Teachers of Mathematics has made a concerted effort to produce standards in school mathematics. Beginning in 1980 with *An Agenda for Action: Recommendations for School Mathematics for the 1980s,* the Council has led a natural progression through *Curriculum and Evaluation Standards for School Mathematics* and *Professional Standards for Teaching Mathematics* to the present *Assessment Standards for School Mathematics.* With the publication of this last volume in the trilogy, the Council has stated clearly what its members, including classroom teachers, supervisors, and college professors, value in curriculum, teaching, and assessment. Thus, it extends the vision of a significant mathematics education for every child.

The Council acknowledges with gratitude the responses of more than two thousand colleagues who thoughtfully reviewed the initial draft. We appreciate greatly the outstanding leadership of Thomas A. Romberg, who chaired the Commission on the Assessment Standards and who effectively guided the final writing process through revisions based on those responses. We are particularly grateful to the working groups, their leaders, and the writers, who deserve great credit for their efforts in translating the concerns and suggestions into reality and who created a document that is user-friendly and an excellent complement to the earlier volumes.

We appreciate the support and contribution of the headquarters staff and particularly Executive Director James Gates, who guided the process and who himself has been involved from the beginning. To each person who had a hand in developing this document we give our heartfelt thanks.

F. Joe Crosswhite, President 1984–86
John A. Dossey, President 1986–88
Shirley M. Frye, President 1988–90
Iris M. Carl, President 1990–92
Mary M. Lindquist, President 1992–94
Jack Price, President 1994–96

PREFACE

In 1992, the National Council of Teachers of Mathematics (NCTM) decided to undertake the development of this document, *Assessment Standards for School Mathematics,* to complement its earlier *Standards* documents, *Curriculum and Evaluation Standards for School Mathematics* (1989) and *Professional Standards for Teaching Mathematics* (1991). In early 1993, management and other working group members were appointed to prepare this document. A first draft was completed in August of that summer. Then, during the 1993–94 school year, critiques and comments were received from more than two thousand reviewers. In particular, the members of the Resource Group were asked for specific comments on the draft and suggestions for its revision. Their input has helped ensure that this document represents the broader views of the educational community. During the summer, fall, and winter of 1994–95, the document was revised, edited, and produced.

The authors of these Assessment Standards (see page v of this report) include K–12 classroom teachers, mathematics educators, educational psychologists, mathematics supervisors, and administrators. Some of them participated in the development of the earlier *Standards* documents for NCTM; several have been involved in the development of alternative assessments at the state level; some have been active researchers investigating new assessment procedures; a number of the authors have participated in other innovative projects, and most have been involved with new classroom, school, district, or state or provincial assessments. These experiences are reflected in the diversity and richness of the examples and vignettes that have been included to illustrate specific assessment purposes. Thus, we represent a cross section of members of NCTM, and the messages in this document are intended to represent the work of school mathematics teachers committed to NCTM's vision of reform in the content, teaching, and learning of school mathematics.

This document is based on extensive recent research and developments related to national efforts to reform the teaching and learning of mathematics. (See References and Selected Assessment Bibliography at the end of this document.) In particular, a recent report from the Mathematical Sciences Education Board (MSEB), *Measuring What Counts* (1993), provided an initial scholarly base for the development of these Assessment Standards.

We thank all who contributed their comments on the draft version of these standards. Their careful reviews and thoughtful suggestions have been of great assistance in the completion of this document.

INTRODUCTION

The *Assessment Standards for School Mathematics* has been produced by the National Council of Teachers of Mathematics (NCTM) because we believe new assessment strategies and practices need to be developed that will enable teachers and others to assess students' performance in a manner that reflects the NCTM's reform vision for school mathematics. Our vision includes the mathematics we expect students to know and be able to use, the way they have learned it, and how their progress is to be assessed. For school assessment practices to inform educators as they progress toward this vision, it is essential that we move away from the "rank order of achievement" approach in assessment toward an approach that is philosophically consistent with NCTM's vision of school mathematics and classroom instruction.

At present, a new approach to assessment is evolving in many schools and classrooms. Instead of assuming that the purpose of assessment is to rank students on a particular trait, the new approach assumes that high public expectations can be set that every student can strive for and achieve, that different performances can and will meet agreed-on expectations, and that teachers can be fair and consistent judges of diverse student performances. Setting high expectations and striving to achieve them are quite different from comparing students with one another and indicating where each student ranks. A constant theme of this document is that decisions regarding students' achievement should be made on the basis of a convergence of information from a variety of balanced and equitable sources. Furthermore, much of the information needs to be derived by teachers during the process of instruction. Teachers are the persons who are in the best position to judge the development of students' progress and, hence, must be considered the primary assessors of students. However, depending on the purpose, there are other assessors, such as learners who assess their own progress.

Background to the Assessment Standards

NCTM's earlier *Standards* documents—*Curriculum and Evaluation Standards for School Mathematics* and *Professional Standards for Teaching Mathematics*—presented a vision of appropriate mathematical goals for all students. This vision, based on the assumption that *all students are capable of learning mathematics,* is at the heart of the NCTM's reform efforts. In the past, school mathematics was organized and taught, and students' performance assessed, in a way that underestimated the mathematical capability of most students and perpetuated costly myths about students' ability and effort. Too often, tests designed for other purposes have been used unintentionally as filters that deny underrepresented groups access to the further study of mathematics. Today, the mathematical development of each child in a diverse multicultural society must be valued. Assessment procedures must no longer be used to deny students the opportunity to learn important mathematics. Instead, assessment should be a means of fostering growth toward high expectations. To do otherwise represents a waste of human potential.

These Assessment Standards have been designed to expand on and complement, not replace, the NCTM's Evaluation Standards. The Evaluation Standards proposed that

◆ student assessment be aligned with, and integral to, instruction;

Assessment needs to reflect the reform vision of school mathematics.

Teachers are in the best position to judge students' progress.

All students are capable of learning mathematics, and their learning can be assessed.

Assessment should be a means of fostering growth toward high expectations.

These Assessment Standards have been designed to expand on and complement the NCTM's Evaluation Standards.

◆ multiple sources of assessment information be used;

◆ assessment methods be appropriate for their purposes;

◆ all aspects of mathematical knowledge and its connections be assessed;

◆ instruction and curriculum be considered equally in judging the quality of a program.

These Assessment Standards establish additional criteria for student assessment and program evaluation and elaborate the vision of assessment that was described in the Evaluation Standards.

If NCTM's vision is to be realized, all aspects of school mathematics—content, teaching, and assessment—need to change on a systemic basis. Included in this vision are the following:

Shift in content:

**Toward** a rich variety of mathematical topics and problem situations
**Away** from just arithmetic

◆ A shift in the mathematical content that students are expected to learn. This shift reflects the belief that all students need the opportunity to develop an understanding of algebra, geometry, trigonometry, statistics, probability, discrete mathematics, and even calculus. This vision implies that high expectations need to be publicly set for all students. Thus, the vision of a reform curriculum is toward a balanced variety of rich problem situations that encourage students to make connections among the various mathematical topics and that reflect cultural diversity. This shift is away from considering arithmetic proficiency as sufficient mathematics for most students.

Shift in learning:

**Toward** investigating problems
**Away** from memorizing and repeating

◆ A shift in the vision of learning mathematics toward investigating, formulating, representing, reasoning, and applying a variety of strategies to the solution of problems—then reflecting on these uses of mathematics—and away from being shown or told, memorizing, and repeating. This represents a shift from mechanical to cognitive work and also assumes the acquisition of a healthy disposition toward mathematics. Furthermore, cognitive work for all students is culturally dependent because students bring to each lesson their past experiences and the diverse facets of their cultural identities. Thus, instruction that capitalizes, and builds, on what students bring to a problem situation can motivate them to struggle with, and make sense of, the problem and share their thinking with classmates.

Shift in teaching:

**Toward** questioning and listening
**Away** from telling

◆ A shift in the role of teachers toward "questioning and listening" as their classrooms become stimulating intellectual learning communities and away from "telling" students what to do. High expectations, challenging work, strong effort, mutual respect, and assistance in supporting the achievement of all students characterize exemplary classrooms in NCTM's vision.

Shift in evaluation:

**Toward** evidence from several sources judged by teachers
**Away** from a single test judged externally

◆ A shift in the vision of evaluation toward a system based on evidence from multiple sources and away from relying on evidence from a single test as well as a shift toward relying on the professional judgments of teachers and away from using only externally derived evidence.

In NCTM's _Standards_ documents, the phrase _mathematical power_ has been used to capture the shift in expectations for all students. The shift is toward understanding concepts and skills; drawing on mathematical concepts and skills when confronted with both routine and nonroutine problems; communicating effectively about the strategies, reasoning, and results of mathematical investigations; and becoming confident in using mathematics to make sense of real-life situations. It is away from mastering a large collection of concepts and skills in a particular order. In this document, the terms *know, know how, be able to do,* and *disposition toward* are used as indicators for the complexity of *mathematical power.*

Shift in expectations:
Toward *using concepts and procedures to solve problems*
Away *from just mastering isolated concepts and procedures*

Many schools and teachers have responded enthusiastically to the *Curriculum and Evaluation Standards* and the *Professional Teaching Standards* by changing both the mathematical content of their courses and the way in which the content is taught. As schools and teachers change their practices, they face the dilemma that the result of their efforts to meet new goals may not be supported by traditional assessment practices because such practices are inconsistent with these new views of mathematics and how learning progresses. The Assessment Standards presented in this document reflect the values and goals associated with the type of assessment system that must be achieved if the reforms envisioned in the teaching and learning of mathematics are to become a reality. We challenge teachers, school district personnel, and state or provincial officials to read and reflect on these standards, critically examine their own current assessment systems, and then work to develop new systems that are consistent with the reform vision.

However, this document is not meant to be construed as a "how to" document. Consistent with the philosophy underlying the earlier *Standards* publications, the ideas presented here are intended to guide teachers and others as they examine current assessment practices and plan new assessment systems. As with the previous *Standards* publications, NCTM will continue to develop companion publications to respond to specific assessment issues.

The Assessment Standards *is a guide, not a "how to" document.*

Mathematics Assessment

In this document, *assessment* is defined as *the process of gathering evidence about a student's knowledge of, ability to use, and disposition toward, mathematics and of making inferences from that evidence for a variety of purposes.* (Important terms used in these pages are defined in the Glossary; definitions have been provided to clarify terms that may have other colloquial meanings or technical meaning in the assessment literature.)

Assessment *is the process of gathering evidence about a student's knowledge of, ability to use, and disposition toward, mathematics and of making inferences from that evidence for a variety of purposes.*

Furthermore, by *evaluation* we mean *the process of determining the worth of, or assigning a value to, something on the basis of careful examination and judgment.* The term *evaluation* as used in this document refers to one use of assessment information. The focus on gathering evidence and making inferences emphasizes that assessment is a process of describing what mathematics students know and can do.

Evaluation *refers to the process of determining the worth of, or assigning a value to, something on the basis of careful examination and judgment.*

There are many audiences for, or consumers of, assessment data as well as different purposes for assessments. For example, every student is well aware of being assessed while in school. In any given mathematics class, some student is bound to ask, "Will this be on the test?" Students have learned that what is assessed and how it is assessed reflect what educators value. It is only reasonable that students should know how they are to be assessed, what mathematics they will be expected to do, the criteria for judging their performance, and the consequences of the assessment, and they have the right to receive timely feedback on their performance. Teachers' responsibilities, in large part, involve judging students' performance during the classroom lesson, students' progress throughout a unit of instruction, and students' knowledge and competence at various points during a semester or year. Also, the public has a need and right to know how well students are performing in schools. Information on students' performance is used to indicate the comparative status of students, schools, districts, and even states and provinces. Summary performance data are also used to evaluate students' achievement, to evaluate programs, and to make policy decisions. Judgments of students' progress, instructional decisions, and evaluations of instructional programs must be based on reasonable interpretations of high-quality, relevant evidence.

Assessment involves several interrelated, but nonsequential, phases.

The assessment process can be thought of as four interrelated phases that highlight principal points at which critical decisions need to be made. Figure 1 shows the four phases—plan the assessment, gather evidence, interpret the evidence, and use the results. The division is arbitrary, however, and makes the process seem more orderly than it actually is. In practice, the phases are interactive, and the distinctions between them are blurred. Assessment does not proceed through them in a neat, linear fashion.

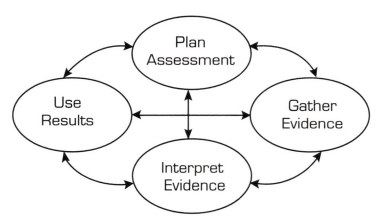

Fig. 1. Four phases of assessment

The phases should also not be seen as necessarily sequential. Rather, they should serve as markers to be used as a guide. Each phase of the assessment process can be characterized by the decisions and actions that occur within that phase as follows:

The four phases of assessment can be characterized by the decisions and actions that occur during them.

Planning the assessment

♦ What purpose does the assessment serve?

♦ What framework is used to give focus and balance to the activities?

♦ What methods are used for gathering and interpreting evidence?

♦ What criteria are used for judging performances on activities?

♦ What formats are used for summarizing judgments and reporting results?

Gathering evidence

- How are activities and tasks created or selected?
- How are procedures selected for engaging students in the activities?
- How are methods for creating and preserving evidence of the performances to be judged?

Interpreting the evidence

- How is the quality of the evidence determined?
- How is an understanding of the performances to be inferred from the evidence?
- What specific criteria are applied to judge the performances?
- Have the criteria been applied appropriately?
- How will the judgments be summarized as results?

Using the results

- How will the results be reported?
- How should inferences from the results be made?
- What action will be taken based on the inferences?
- How can it be ensured that these results will be incorporated in subsequent instruction and assessment?

An assessor might be a student assessing his or her own progress in learning probability, a teacher developing assessment activities for a unit on decimals, a district committee choosing among performance assessments in algebra, a state or provincial mathematics supervisor analyzing data from a collection of student portfolios, or a major test publisher developing an instrument to evaluate a course on applications of mathematics. Whatever the assessment, whoever the assessor, the assessment process itself includes some combination of decisions and actions drawn from the four phases. The phrase *assessment process* and the diagram in figure 1 are used in this document to emphasize the complex process that underlies the purposes for which assessments are done, the decisions made by the assessors, and the standards to which assessments are held. This vision of assessment should apply to any assessment purpose.

This Document

This document presents six assessment standards that are the criteria to be used for judging assessment practices. To illustrate their use, four general categories of educational purposes for which evidence about student performance is commonly gathered are presented. The document concludes with a section entitled "What's Next?" In that section, suggestions are made about using the document, and the reform vision of assessment is summarized. Teachers and other assessors are challenged to examine their current practices, to recognize—and, if necessary, create—the conditions needed for implementing these six standards, and to build new assessment systems consistent with this vision.

Those who serve on school or district-wide mathematics committees will find this document a useful tool in redrafting assessments.

This document can be used by classroom teachers, curriculum directors, and department chairs to guide classroom, school, and district assessment practices; by policymakers and administrators to generate and support needed improvements in mathematical assessments; and by state or provincial and commercial test publishers to align their assessment systems with those of schools or districts in order to provide more useful data to students, teachers, parents, and the public at large. In particular, those who serve on school or district-wide mathematics committees will find this document to be a useful tool in redrafting assessments that align with the vision of curricula and teaching outlined in NCTM's previous *Standards* documents.

Finally, we suggest that all of us continue to consider, study, and work to apply the ideas presented in the three NCTM *Standards* documents, addenda, and other resources in our effort to examine current curriculum, instructional, and assessment practices. By doing so, we can continue to develop new assessment systems that support the changes in content and instruction envisioned by NCTM.

In order to develop mathematical power in all *students, assessment needs to support the continued mathematics learning of* each *student.*

In order to develop mathematical power in *all* students, assessment needs to support the continued mathematics learning of *each* student. This is the central goal of assessment in school mathematics. In our view, assessment occurs at the intersection of important mathematics content, teaching practices, and student learning. Assessment that embodies the vision of the six standards presented here will be a dynamic process that informs teachers, students, and others and supports each student's continuing growth in mathematical power.

MATHEMATICS ASSESSMENT STANDARDS

The standards presented in this section provide criteria for judging the quality of mathematics assessments. They are statements about what is valued. Together, they reflect a vision of exemplary mathematics assessment.

As individuals and groups face assessment decisions, attention to the standards presented here should enable them to create a high-quality assessment process. Why so few standards? Why these six? To be useful, the standards need to be limited in number yet comprehensive enough to cover major issues of mathematics assessment. They address *mathematics, learning, equity, openness, inferences,* and *coherence.* Focus questions are provided to facilitate the application of each standard—that is, the questions are intended to help in determining the extent to which a specific mathematics assessment meets the standard.

All six standards apply to all mathematics assessments. They can be applied to specific assessment activities or to an entire assessment system. The Coherence Standard differs from the others, connecting them to the assessment system and to the purposes for which assessment is done.

The Assessment Standards promote the dynamic and ongoing process of improving mathematics curricula, mathematics teaching, and mathematics assessment. The process involves everyone concerned with mathematics education. These standards for assessment contribute to, and are affected by, the standards for curriculum and the standards for teaching.

The Assessment Standards provide criteria for judging the quality of mathematics assessments.

THE MATHEMATICS STANDARD

Assessment should reflect the mathematics that all students need to know and be able to do.

The NCTM *Curriculum and Evaluation Standards for School Mathematics* presents a vision of the mathematics that all students need to know and be able to do. Mathematics and its uses in society continue to grow and change. Therefore, the mathematics taught in schools continues to evolve.

From time to time, mathematics teachers attempt to formulate a statement about the school mathematics curriculum based on current understanding of mathematics and mathematics learning. The *Curriculum and Evaluation Standards* is the most recent in a series of such statements. It represents the best of contemporary thinking concerning not only the mathematics topics that students need to learn but also the important ways in which mathematical knowledge is learned and used. It reflects a shift in the importance that the world outside the schools increasingly places on thinking and problem solving. Procedural skills alone do not prepare students for that world. Therefore, students deserve a curriculum that develops their mathematical power and an assessment system that enables them to show it.

Assessments that match the current vision of school mathematics involve activities that are based on significant and correct mathematics. These activities provide all students with opportunities to formulate problems, reason mathematically, make connections among mathematical ideas, and communicate about mathematics. Students engage in solving realistic problems using information and the technological tools available in real life. Moreover, skills, procedural knowledge, and factual knowledge are assessed as part of the doing of mathematics. In fact, these skills are best assessed in the same way they are used, as tools for performing mathematically significant tasks.

Possessing mathematical power includes being able, and predisposed, to apply mathematical understanding in new situations, as well as having the confidence to do so. A comprehensive program of mathematics assessment includes opportunities for students to show what they can do with mathematics that they may not have studied formally but that they are prepared to investigate. Some assessments may be designed to determine how well students, presented with an unfamiliar situation, can use what they have learned previously. Other assessments may require that students learn a new mathematical concept or strategy during the assessment and use this knowledge to solve problems. Assessors need to recognize, too, that the mathematical ideas elicited by an assessment activity are not always those that are intended. Students respond to open activities in creative ways, and their responses should be judged according to the quality of the mathematics demonstrated.

Developing assessment activities that reflect mathematics all students should know and be able to do requires that assessors understand

All students need to know and be able to do the mathematics emphasized by the Curriculum and Evaluation Standards.

"Assessment should reflect the mathematics that it is most important for students to learn."
—Mathematical Sciences Education Board (1993, p. 32)

See the example "A Middle-Grades Statistics Unit" on page 30 for an example of using computers as tools in the assessment of realistic problem solving.

See the example "Judging Progress Equitably" on page 36 for an example of an assessment task that encourages students to continue exploring and learning.

The examples "Changing Plans in Mid-Lesson" on page 47 and "Selecting Appropriate Instructional Experiences" on page 52 illustrate how teachers use their understanding of mathematics, their familiarity with the curriculum, and their knowledge of how students learn in their assessments.

mathematics, be familiar with mathematics curricula, and know how students learn. Documents such as the *Curriculum and Evaluation Standards* and *Professional Teaching Standards* can help, but they cannot prescribe an assessment program for each student. Decisions about assessments should be made in consultation with colleagues and take into account the experiences of the students being assessed.

An assessment framework that gives appropriate weight to different facets of mathematics presents a comprehensive view of the mathematics that is important for students to know and be able to do. A specific assessment activity makes sense only within such a framework. A range of assessments that fit into the framework not only gives students multiple opportunities to display their developing mathematical power but also increases their opportunities to learn additional mathematics. Constructing an assessment framework helps ensure that the mathematics assessed over a school year, as well as throughout each student's school experience, forms a balanced, integrated whole.

To determine how well an assessment reflects mathematics that students need to know and be able to do, ask questions such as the following:

♦ What mathematics is reflected in the assessment?

♦ What efforts are made to ensure that the mathematics is significant and correct?

♦ How does the assessment engage students in realistic and worthwhile mathematical activities?

♦ How does the assessment elicit the use of mathematics that it is important to know and be able to do?

♦ How does the assessment fit within a framework of mathematics to be assessed?

♦ What inferences about students' mathematical knowledge, understanding, thinking processes, and dispositions can be made from the assessment?

For an example of how assessment tasks and scoring criteria are related to underlying curricular and assessment frameworks, see "A Balanced Assessment System" on page 60.

THE LEARNING STANDARD

Assessment should enhance mathematics learning.

As an integral part of mathematics instruction, assessment contributes significantly to all students' learning. Because students learn mathematics while being assessed, assessments are learning opportunities as well as opportunities for students to demonstrate what they know and can do. Moreover, assessments, including those external to the classroom, guide subsequent instruction, and thus they can further enhance students' learning. Students can also themselves use assessments to become independent learners. They can do so by using assessments as indicators of the mathematics important for them to learn. Although assessment is done for a variety of reasons, its main goal is to advance students' learning and inform teachers as they make instructional decisions.

Assessment is a communication process in which assessors—whether students themselves, teachers, or others—learn something about what students know and can do and in which students learn something about what assessors value. When the focus and form of assessment are different from that of instruction, assessment subverts students' learning by sending them conflicting messages about what mathematics is valued. When instruction pursues one set of goals and the assessment—especially if it is for high stakes—pursues another, students are faced with a dilemma and must assume that the goals of assessment are the ones that count.

Assessment that enhances mathematics learning becomes a routine part of ongoing classroom activity rather than an interruption. Assessment does not simply mark the end of a learning cycle. Rather, it is an integral part of instruction that encourages and supports further learning. Opportunities for informal assessment occur naturally in every lesson. They include listening to students, observing them, and making sense of what they say and do. Especially with very young children, the observation of students' work can reveal qualities of thinking not tapped by written or oral activities. In planning lessons and making instructional decisions, teachers identify opportunities for a variety of assessments. Questions like the following become a regular part of the teacher's planning: "What questions will I ask?" "What will I observe?" "What activities are likely to provide me with information about students' learning?" Preparation for a formal assessment does not mean stopping regular instruction and teaching to the test. Instead, for students, ongoing instruction is the best preparation for assessment. Similarly, for teachers, ongoing assessment is the best foundation for instruction.

Assessment that enhances mathematics learning incorporates activities that are consistent with, and sometimes the same as, the activities used in instruction. For example, if students are learning by communicating their mathematical ideas in writing, their knowledge of mathematics is assessed, in part, by having them write about their mathematical ideas. If they are learning in groups, they may be assessed in groups. If graphing calculators are used in instruction, they are to be available for use in assessment.

Although assessment is done for a variety of reasons, its main goal is to advance students' learning and inform teachers as they make instructional decisions.

"It is through our assessment that we communicate most clearly to students which activities and learning outcomes we value."

—David J. Clarke
(1989, p.1)

For examples of assessment integrated with instruction, see "Listening to Students" on page 32 and "Using Evidence to Plan Tomorrow's Lesson" on page 49.

"In order for assessment to support student learning, it must include teachers in all stages of the process and be embedded in curriculum and teaching activities."

—Linda Darling-Hammond
(1994, p. 25)

See "Selecting Appropriate Instructional Experiences" on page 52 for an example of using classroom work products as assessment evidence.

For an example of how students acquire an understanding of assessment criteria, see "A Middle-Grades Statistics Unit" on page 30.

For an example of self- and peer-assessment, see "Learning to Judge One's Own Work" on page 39.

"The assessment of students' mathematical disposition should seek information about their inclination to monitor and reflect on their own thinking and performance."
—NCTM (1989, p. 233)

Students' classroom work, along with projects and other out-of-class work, is a rich source of assessment data for making inferences about students' learning. Many products of classroom activity are indicators of mathematics learning: oral comments, written papers, journal entries, drawings, computer-generated models, and other means of representing knowledge. Students and teachers use this evidence, along with information from more formal assessment activities, to determine next steps in learning. Evidence of mathematics learning can be found in activities that range from draft work, through work that reflects students' use of feedback and helpful criticism, to a polished end product. Continuous assessment of students' work not only facilitates their learning of mathematics but also enhances their confidence in what they understand and can communicate. Moreover, external assessments support instruction most strongly when classroom work is included. When classroom work, the teacher's judgments, and students' reflections are valued parts of an external assessment, they enhance students' mathematics learning by increasing the fit between instructional goals and assessment.

If students are to function as independent learners, they must reflect on their progress, understand what they know and can do, be confident in their learning, and ascertain what they have yet to learn. When students work as partners with teachers and peers in the assessment process, they learn to monitor their progress in learning. Teachers help students become independent self-assessors by providing sample tasks and sample criteria for judging responses, by describing how the tasks and criteria were created, and by showing how the criteria are applied. Students can create tasks, develop criteria of their own, and apply the criteria to their work and to the work of others. As the shift from teacher-centered to student-centered classrooms occurs, students become more active participants in assessment. In these classrooms, students learn to reflect on their work and their learning, make critical self-judgments, critique the work of their peers, and use productively the critiques of others.

To determine how well an assessment enhances learning, ask questions such as these:

♦ How does the assessment contribute to each student's learning of mathematics?

♦ How does the assessment relate to instruction?

♦ How does the assessment allow students to demonstrate what they know and what they can do in novel situations?

♦ How does the assessment engage students in relevant, purposeful work on worthwhile mathematical activities?

♦ How does the assessment build on each student's understanding, interests, and experiences?

♦ How does the assessment involve students in selecting activities, applying performance criteria, and using results?

♦ How does the assessment provide opportunities for students to evaluate, reflect on, and improve their own work—that is, to become independent learners?

THE EQUITY STANDARD

Assessment should promote equity.

Equitable practices in assessment benefit everyone by focusing attention on *each* student's learning. For each student, equitable assessment practices raise expectations, clarify what mathematics is, and help that student learn. Equitable practices honor each student's unique qualities and experiences. Adherence to an equity standard means that all students, including those with special needs or talents, are expected to reach high levels of accomplishment. It also means that each student is given opportunities to reach those levels and the necessary support to do so. Although professionals may disagree on ways and means of achieving equity, its place as a goal is not in doubt. It is not to be ignored or devalued. Equitable assessment practices help to increase equity throughout the educational system.

In the past we wanted all students to learn some mathematics, but we differentiated among the types of mathematics education different groups of students received. Now we have high expectations for all students, envisioning a mathematics education that develops each student's mathematical power to the fullest.

In an equitable assessment, each student has an opportunity to demonstrate his or her mathematical power. Because different students show what they know and can do in different ways, assessments should allow for multiple approaches. Sometimes different assessments or combinations of assessments are used to provide evidence of the same mathematics learning. When students have special needs, provision is made to ensure that they can demonstrate their understanding. For example, assessors use English-enhancing and bilingual techniques to support students who are learning English. Assessment is equitable when students with special needs or talents have access to the same accommodations and modifications they receive in instruction.

Assessments have too often ignored differences in students' experience, physical condition, gender, and ethnic, cultural, and social backgrounds in an effort to be fair. This practice has led to assessments that do not take differences among students into account. The experiences each student brings to any classroom and to any assessment are unique. Students' knowledge and ways of thinking and learning about mathematics are a complex integration of their backgrounds with their experiences in school. Equitable judgments about students' mathematics learning reflect the ways in which their unique qualities influence how they learn mathematics and how they communicate that knowledge. Students' backgrounds and experiences influence how they perceive an assessment situation and may cause them to respond in unanticipated ways. Students may need to specify the assumptions they are making when they communicate the results of their work. Assessors need to be open to alternative solutions. Probing what students are thinking, being sensitive to their experiences, and understanding how they perceive the assessment situation all contribute to making equitable decisions about students' learning.

"Assessments can contribute to students' opportunities to learn important mathematics only if they reflect, and are reinforced by, high expectations for every student."
—Mathematical Sciences Education Board (1993, p. 109)

We envision a mathematics education that develops each student's mathematical power to the fullest.

See the example "Judging Progress Equitably" on page 36 for an illustration of assessment that allows all students to demonstrate their knowledge.

The example "Listening to Students" on page 32 provides an example of assessment that considers students' unique problem-solving strategies.

"Different cultural groups in U.S. society may have different intellectual traditions that create different conceptions of reality than that tapped by our testing instruments."
—George F. Madaus (1994, p. 80)

See the example "Understanding Variations in Performance" on page 73, which illustrates the examination of subsets of group data.

Assessment results are also powerful tools for monitoring—at the class-room, school, district, or state or provincial level—whether all students are provided equitable opportunities to learn important mathematics. Ideally, the results will reveal no systematic differences in performance that can be connected with characteristics unrelated to mathematics learning. When such differences are found, educators determine whether they have resulted from inequitable opportunities either to learn or to demonstrate learning. In the latter case, assessments can furnish information to guide meaningful action by learners, teachers, and other educators toward remedying the inequity. The burden for taking action to ensure equitable opportunities both for teachers to teach and for students to learn and to show their learning rests on the entire educational system.

"Prior knowledge, experience, and the opportunity to learn are important considerations in interpreting test results."
—NCTM (1989, p. 202)

Teachers and other professionals also bring different perspectives to the assessment process. In their role as assessors, they need opportunities to become informed about the norms and values of different racial, ethnic, cultural, gender, and social groups. In responding to the needs of the students they are assessing, however, teachers and others should recognize that each student is a unique member of many groups and is not to be stereotyped. Assessors sensitive to equity are willing to acknowledge and compensate for their personal biases. Even in seemingly homogeneous settings, assessors are constantly aware that students' views and interpretations may differ considerably from their own. Teachers, other professionals, parents, and community members with appropriate background and experience can provide rich insights into students' perspectives.

Equity poses many challenges to assessment. Assessments have traditionally ignored differences, and consequently their results have excluded some students from opportunities to learn important mathematics. Assessment results have also had little value in determining and supporting instruction for certain students. An equitable assessment process is important for removing these injustices. Equity is not a concern for some students; it is a concern for all.

To determine how well an assessment promotes equity, ask questions such as the following:

- What opportunities has each student had to learn the mathematics being assessed?
- How does the assessment provide alternative activities or modes of response that invite each student to engage in the mathematics being assessed?
- How does the design of the assessment enable all students to exhibit what they know and can do?
- How do the conditions under which the assessment is administered enable all students to exhibit what they know and can do?
- How does the assessment help students demonstrate their best work?
- How is the role of students' backgrounds and experiences recognized in judging their responses to the assessment?
- How do scoring guides accommodate unanticipated but reasonable responses?
- How have the effects of bias been minimized throughout the assessment?
- To what sources can differences in performance be attributed?

THE OPENNESS STANDARD

Assessment should be an open process.

Openness in the process of assessment can be assured in several ways. First, information about the process is made available to those affected by it. Before their learning is assessed in a formal way, all students are informed about what they need to know, how they will be expected to demonstrate that knowledge, and what the consequences of assessment will be. They may not know the exact questions they will be asked, but they do know the nature of those questions. They get prompt and useful information about the quality of their work. When students understand the criteria used in judging their work and are shown examples of adequate and inadequate responses, their performance improves. Openness contributes to equitable assessments.

When externally generated assessments are open, students and teachers receive timely information about how the information will be gathered and how the results will be used. The assessments are consistent with the learning goals students are pursuing in class. The results are reported promptly so they can be used in instruction. Sample items, clear statements of performance criteria, and illustrative student work help in the interpretation of the results.

Openness in assessment includes informing the public (parents, policymakers, business and industry leaders, members of the mathematics community, and interested citizens) about the process. The public is given information about the classroom assessments that teachers are using as well as the assessments that are mandated by the district or the state or province. The public has access to samples of scored student work discussed against the background of an assessment framework and, consequently, understands how students are expected to show the mathematics they have learned.

Second, an open assessment process honors professional involvement. In an assessment program—whether for a school, a district, a state or province, or the nation—teachers are active participants in all phases. They participate directly in deciding what is to be assessed and how, developing criteria for performance, selecting students' work to illustrate the criteria, developing procedures for reporting results, and describing intended uses and consequences. An assessment process that is open to participation by teachers helps them form common definitions of the mathematics to be assessed and reach consensus on the appropriate evidence of students' learning. In departments and schools with an open assessment process, teachers meet to discuss learning goals, expectations, students' work, and criteria for evaluating achievement.

A third facet of openness is that the assessment process is open to scrutiny and modification. Mathematics assessment that supports NCTM's visions of the mathematics curriculum and of mathematics teaching will change as those visions evolve. Assessments are continually examined for flaws and continually revised to be in harmony with other reforms.

See the examples "A Middle-Grades Statistics Unit" on page 30 and "Providing Written Feedback on Students' Work" on page 34 for illustrations of openness with assessment criteria.

See the examples "Program Selection" on page 69 and "Using Assessment to Meet Students' Needs" on page 75 for examples of the professional involvement of teachers.

Developing new performance criteria needs to be an open process. See the example "Rethinking the Meaning of Grades" on page 57 for an illustration.

Everyone is best served by an assessment process that is public, participatory, and dynamic.

Open review of the assessment process means that everyone who is affected by the assessment of students' learning obtains sufficient information in order to provide appropriate input. Public consensus on performance criteria develops out of a criterion-setting process. The consensus is balanced against considerations of diversity in the process so that students continue to have multiple means and opportunities to demonstrate their mathematical power.

Open assessment involves shared responsibilities by students, teachers, and the public. It contributes to a collective understanding of high performance criteria for mathematics and strives to narrow the gap between students' current performance and their attainment of those criteria. Everyone is best served by an assessment process that is public, participatory, and dynamic.

To determine how open an assessment is, ask questions such as these:

♦ How do students become familiar with the assessment process and with the purposes, performance criteria, and consequences of the assessment?

♦ How are teachers and students involved in choosing tasks, setting criteria, and interpreting results?

♦ How is the public involved in the assessment process?

♦ What access do those affected by the assessment have to tasks, scoring goals, performance criteria, and samples of students' work that have been scored and discussed?

♦ How is the assessment process itself open to evaluation and modification?

THE INFERENCES STANDARD

Assessment should promote valid inferences about mathematics learning.

Assessment is a process of gathering evidence and of making inferences from that evidence for various purposes. The primary technical question involves defining procedures for making valid inferences from evidence of a student's learning. An inference about learning is a conclusion about a student's cognitive processes that cannot be observed directly. The conclusion has to be based instead on the student's performance. Many potential sources of performance are available. Mathematics assessment includes evidence from observations, interviews, open-ended tasks, extended problem situations, and portfolios as well as more traditional instruments such as multiple-choice and short-answer tests.

A valid inference is based on evidence that is adequate and relevant. Valid inferences also depend on informed judgment on the part of whoever interprets and uses the evidence. Teachers make instructional decisions daily that are based on inferences they have made about students' learning. They use their professional judgment in examining relevant evidence. The validity of their inferences depends on their expertise and the quality of the assessment evidence they have gathered. Similarly, valid inferences from large-scale assessments require relevant evidence and are based on the best professional judgment.

Using multiple sources of evidence can improve the validity of the inferences made about students' learning. The *Curriculum and Evaluation Standards* urges that decisions concerning students' learning be based on a convergence of evidence from a variety of sources. The use of multiple sources allows strengths in one source to compensate for weaknesses in others. It also helps teachers judge the consistency of students' mathematical work.

A threat to the validity of inferences comes from potential bias in the evidence. New forms of assessment, such as portfolios or extended projects, may create new sources of bias. Extended projects may allow students to complete some of the work at home, with the result that differences in home resources (including assistance from parents) may bias the results. To ensure the equality of resources, additional materials may have to be provided at school or in the community so that all students can do the projects to the best of their ability. Another source of potential bias lies in assessment activities that rely heavily on students' ability to use the English language to communicate mathematical knowledge. This bias can be addressed through additional activities that allow alternative forms of communication. A third source of bias may derive from the forms of scoring used in many assessment activities. Complex tasks require considerable judgment by the scorers. Bias in that judgment is addressed through suitable training and scoring procedures. Involving individuals with relevant expertise not only helps guard against biased scores but also contributes to equity and openness by offering diverse perspectives.

An inference about learning is a conclusion about a student's cognitive processes that cannot be observed directly. The conclusion has to be based instead on the student's performance.

A valid inference requires evidence that is adequate and relevant.

The examples "Changing Plans in Mid-Lesson" on page 47 and "Using Evidence to Plan Tomorrow's Lesson" on page 49 offer illustrations of instructional decisions based on valid inferences of students' learning.

"Analyzing Scores" on page 71 is an example of inferences made from large-scale assessments.

See "A Middle-Grades Statistics Unit" on page 30 for an example of the use of multiple sources of evidence for assessment.

"An exclusive reliance on a single type of assessment can frustrate students, diminish their self-confidence, and make them feel anxious about, or antagonistic toward, mathematics."
—NCTM (1989, p. 202)

The example "A Balanced Assessment System" on page 60 illustrates a high-stakes assessment that results in certification.

Inferences about mathematics learning have various consequences. Some inferences affect what students study tomorrow; others affect whether they graduate. Regardless of the consequences, the validity of each inference must be established. The amount and type of evidence that is needed, however, depends on the consequences of the inference. On the one hand, an informal interview of a student can provide a teacher with sufficient evidence of a student's progress to enable the teacher to determine what mathematical task is most appropriate for the student to engage in next. On the other hand, a large-scale, high-stakes assessment where results are used for certification or a culminating experience in school mathematics requires much more evidence and a more formal analysis of that evidence.

New forms of assessment require increased attention to the procedures for making valid inferences about the mathematics that students know and can do. Assessments that are based on a framework of important mathematics, draw on multiple sources of evidence, minimize bias, and support students' learning provide the evidence needed for such inferences. Technical considerations relating to validity, evidence, and inferences should be thought of not as barriers to the use of new and interesting assessments but rather as opportunities to enhance the instructional benefits of assessment.

To determine how well an assessment promotes valid inferences, ask questions such as the following:

◆ What evidence about learning does the assessment provide?

◆ How is professional judgment used in making inferences about learning?

◆ How sensitive is the assessor to the demands the assessment makes and to unexpected responses?

◆ How is bias minimized in making inferences about learning?

◆ What efforts are made to ensure that scoring is consistent across students, scorers, and activities?

◆ What multiple sources of evidence are used for making inferences, and how is the evidence used?

◆ What is the value of the evidence for each use?

THE COHERENCE STANDARD

Assessment should be a coherent process.

Coherence in assessment involves three types of agreement. First, the assessment process forms a coherent whole; the phases fit together. Second, the assessment matches the purposes for which it is being done. When the design, evidence-gathering, evidence-interpreting, and action phases of the assessment process are consistent with one another and with the purposes of the assessment, it has educational value. Third, the assessment is aligned with the curriculum and with instruction. Students' learning connects with their assessment experiences.

A coherent mathematics assessment system assures that assessors will develop activities and performance criteria tailored to the purposes of each assessment. An assessment framework is useful in judging whether all parts of the process are in harmony, from the design stage to the stage of reporting and using results. The assessment process then unfolds as a logical and coherent whole.

The Coherence Standard has several implications. Just as no single instrument section makes a great orchestra, a coherent mathematics assessment system cannot be based on paper-and-pencil tests alone. Instead, a balance among appropriate and diverse assessment activities can help all students learn.

A coherent mathematics assessment system requires that activities be chosen that are appropriate to the purpose at hand. A teacher would not use a test on linear equations to assess students' knowledge of quadratic equations, or a test of procedural skills to indicate students' conceptual knowledge, or a computation test to assess problem-solving performance.

Coherence in assessment, however, raises broader issues than simply selecting an appropriate test or activity. Coherence relates to all aspects of the assessment process.

External assessment programs are moving away from an extensive reliance on machine-scored multiple-choice items to a greater use of performance tasks and to the use of multiple sources of information. Assessment activities for such programs, however, can be expensive to develop, administer, and score. The programs may entail costs in the form of instructional time taken away from other activities if they are not integrated into instruction. Greater investments of time and funding may be required, which means that people may expect more information from the assessments. As assessment programs change, the pressure to make a single assessment serve multiple purposes is likely to increase. Consequently, special vigilance may be needed to assure that all the uses to which assessment information is being put are in harmony with the purposes of the assessment.

Mathematics teachers organize, conduct, and interpret assessments as part of their ongoing mathematics instruction. When mathematics

This standard connects the other standards to assessment systems, assessment purposes, curriculum, and instruction.

See "A Balanced Assessment System" on page 60 for an example of assessment activities where all students can learn.

"The purpose of an assessment ... should dictate the kinds of questions asked, the methods employed, and the uses of the resulting information."
—NCTM (1989, p. 199)

assessment is a coherent process, teachers and students benefit because they are not confronted by conflicting demands. Attention to coherence underscores the principle that assessment needs to be in step with instruction. When assessment fits the curriculum, students can see that assessment activities not only are related to the mathematics they have learned but also serve clear goals. As students understand how assessment is connected to what they are learning, an increase can be expected in the number of students who will choose to continue their study of mathematics.

"Assessment is the guidance system of education just as standards are the guidance system of reform."
—Mathematical Sciences Education Board (1993, p. 2)

Assessment developers in local and provincial or state agencies play a vital role in making sure that the assessments of students' mathematics learning form a harmonious whole as they progress through school. A single assessment touches only a part of the mathematics that students know and can use, but the totality of the assessments students encounter provides a comprehensive picture of their knowledge, skill, and understanding.

To determine how coherent an assessment process is, ask questions such as these:

♦ How is professional judgment used to ensure that the various parts of the assessment process form a coherent whole?

♦ How do students view the connection between instruction and assessment?

♦ How does the assessment match its purposes with its uses?

♦ How does the assessment match the curriculum and instructional practice?

♦ How can assessment practice inform teachers as they make curriculum decisions and determine their instructional practices?

USE OF THE ASSESSMENT STANDARDS FOR DIFFERENT PURPOSES

This section describes how the standards just presented can be used to critique and improve assessment of the learning of mathematics. The examples and vignettes in this document portray some shifts in assessment practice and in the ways in which teachers and others can use the standards to judge the efficacy of mathematics assessments, improve their quality, and generate ideas for alternative ways of assessing mathematics learning. Except for those identified as adapted from research, the vignettes are fictional illustrations and, although drawn from experience, are not factual accounts.

The Assessment Standards can be used to judge the quality of assessment for different purposes.

The section organizes the diverse purposes for which mathematics assessments are made into four broad categories. Although there are many ways to categorize these purposes, the four selected represent primary areas for the reform of assessment practice. What distinguishes each purpose are the objectives to be achieved and the results to be obtained from the assessment. Figure 2 depicts the four purposes (in the ellipse) and the actions (in the rectangles) that result from the use of assessment data in conjunction with each purpose.

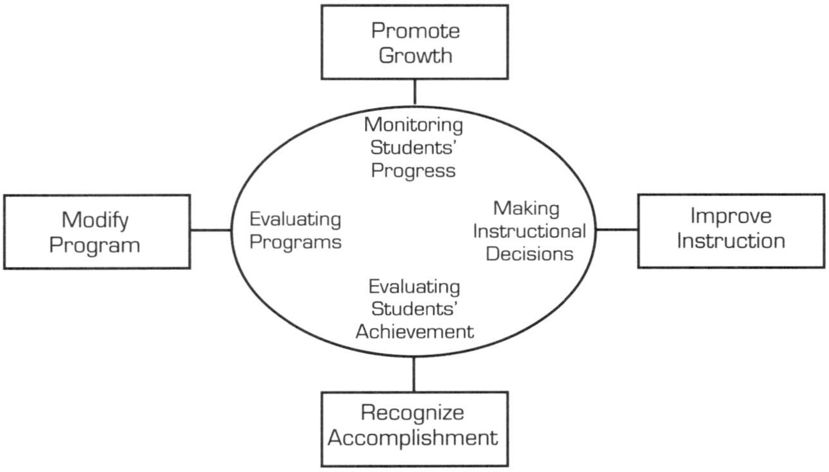

Fig. 2. Four purposes of assessment and their results

One important purpose of assessment is *monitoring students' progress* toward learning goals. After setting high expectations, evidence should be collected to provide each student and the teacher with feedback about progress toward those goals. The feedback is used in an ongoing effort to promote each student's growth in mathematical power. Monitoring is seen as a continuous process. Sometimes the collection of evidence is informal and spontaneous, and sometimes it is formal. Hence, the results are provisional, yet they provide the rich diagnostic feedback important to each student. The basic question to be answered about students' progress is, *How is each student progressing in relation to the goals we have set and agreed on?*

What progress is each student making?

A second and related purpose of mathematics assessment is that of *making instructional decisions.* Teachers use evidence of students' mathematical understanding, along with other evidence from the instructional process, to modify instruction so that it will better facilitate learning. The teacher is the primary assessor of the mathematics that students know and can do. The basic question teachers consider when using assessments undertaken for this purpose is, *How can I use evidence about my students' progress to make instructional decisions?*

What are the appropriate instructional decisions?

A third purpose of mathematics assessment is that of *evaluating students' achievement* at a particular time. At regular intervals, evidence from multiple sources is formally summarized for each student and reported to interested parties. The sources of selected evidence are deliberate, and the reporting is done in a formal manner to acknowledge student achievement publicly and to certify that certain milestones have been reached. The basic question to be answered is, *How does each student's understanding at this time compare with the goals he or she was expected to have achieved?*

Have students reached their goals?

Evaluating programs is a fourth purpose of mathematics assessment. Evidence of students' performance, as well as other data, is used to make decisions about instructional programs so that all students are encouraged to meet high expectations in mathematics. The question being addressed is, *How well is the mathematics program working in relation to goals and expectations for the students?*

Is the program working?

Regardless of the purpose for which they are conducted, all school mathematics assessments envisioned in this document share common features. The six standards apply to each type of assessment. However, the way in which a particular standard is applied in assessments carried out for different purposes may vary.

Several changes in assessment practices are imperative if the practices are to be consistent with curricular and instructional reform efforts. Many current practices furnish incomplete and sometimes biased information about students' mathematical understanding. In each section that follows, three or more shifts in assessment practices are highlighted and illustrated with examples and vignettes. The shifts should be seen as components of needed changes in the total assessment system and not viewed just with respect to the purpose with which they are presented.

Assessment is the shared responsibility of all who are concerned with students' learning of mathematics. The specific educational purposes for which assessments are made have been deliberately chosen to blur the distinction between assessments that are internal to the classroom and assessments that are external. Assessments for monitoring students' progress, making instructional decisions, and evaluating student achievement have typically been the responsibility of classroom teachers, whereas assessments for evaluating programs have been carried out by agencies outside the classroom. The illustrations that follow suggest that assessments for all purposes need to become more open and collegial; that is, teachers need to be involved in the assessment process for all purposes. The primary responsibility for assessment may lie with specific people, depending on the purpose, but it must be a collaborative endeavor if it is to meet the six standards defined in this document.

Information gathered from any source about a student's mathematical understanding is only a sample of the possible information about such understanding. Thus, questions about the sample's representativeness, reliability, and validity must be of concern. Furthermore, for two of the four categories of purposes—*monitoring students' progress* and *evaluating students' achievement*—the sample is of each student's performance, and the information is aggregated to make decisions about that student. For the other two purposes—*making instructional decisions* and *evaluating programs*—the sample represents performance, and the information, although derived from students' performance, is aggregated across students to make other decisions.

All mathematics assessments involve the same four phases—*plan the assessment, gather evidence, interpret the evidence,* and *use the results*—although the aspects of each process that are most crucial may vary with the purpose (see fig. 3). The illustrations in the following sections indicate how the phases of the assessment process relate to assessment purposes and fulfill the intent of the six standards.

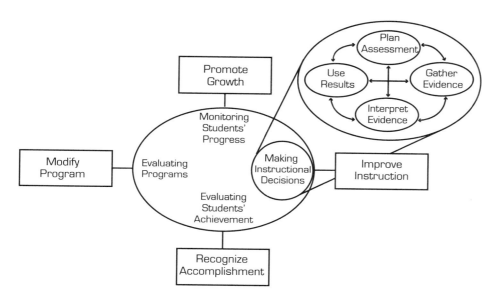

Fig. 3. Relationship between phases of assessment and assessment purposes

The discussion and illustrations of the assessment undertaken for each purpose demonstrate both the shifts in practice and the methods for applying the standards to accomplish those shifts. The discussion shows how the questions for reflection that follow each standard can be used to determine how well specific assessment activities and practices meet the standards under review. The illustrations suggest how those responsible for students' learning of mathematics might begin collectively to apply the standards to specific assessments, thereby making mathematics assessment a more public, open, and collaborative enterprise.

PURPOSE: MONITORING STUDENTS' PROGRESS

Teachers monitor students' progress to understand and document each student's growth in relation to mathematical goals and to provide students with relevant and useful feedback about their work and progress. Goals for students' learning may involve the formulation of long-range or short-range performance criteria. These goals are set in collaboration with students and others responsible for students' learning. Effective monitoring of a student's progress toward those goals enhances learning by clearly communicating what the goals are and the extent to which students have met them.

Teachers have always monitored their students' progress. However, if students are to increase their mathematical power, several related shifts in assessment practice are warranted:

♦ A shift toward judging the progress of each student's attainment of mathematical power, and away from assessing students' knowledge of specific facts and isolated skills

♦ A shift toward communicating with students about their performance in a continuous, comprehensive manner, and away from simply indicating whether or not answers are correct

♦ A shift toward using multiple and complex assessment tools (such as performance tasks, projects, writing assignments, oral demonstrations, and portfolios), and away from sole reliance on answers to brief questions on quizzes and chapter tests

♦ A shift toward students learning to assess their own progress, and away from teachers and external agencies as the sole judges of progress

The primary question to be answered by teachers is, How is each student progressing in relation to the goals we have set and agreed on?

JUDGING PROGRESS TOWARD MATHEMATICAL POWER

The notion of mathematical power, as described in the NCTM *Curriculum and Evaluation Standards for School Mathematics,* includes a student's ability to "explore, conjecture, and reason logically, as well as the ability to use a variety of mathematical methods effectively to solve nonroutine problems" (NCTM 1989, p. 5). Judging progress toward such a complex and broad target involves two components: (1) setting goals in the form of performance criteria, and (2) assessing students' progress toward those goals.

Helping students set and attain goals is at the heart of good teaching. Goals in the reform vision of school mathematics involve collections of related ideas (networks) within and across particular mathematical domains that students are expected to know and use. Each mathematical domain (e.g., addition and subtraction of whole numbers, common fractions, geometry, statistics, functions) includes terms, signs, and symbols; the rules for their use; the situations they commonly represent; and the know-how to use these ideas to solve routine and nonroutine problems.

To assess progress toward the reform goals, performance criteria need to be publicly stated and student performances judged in light of those criteria. There are multiple possible paths toward the achievement of performance criteria, and numerous possible benchmarks and sources of evidence to indicate progress toward it. Furthermore, short-term expectations for individual students may vary because students come to classroom instruction with varying backgrounds, interests, and talents.

Example: A Middle-Grades Statistics Unit

The following vignette illustrates how technology can be used for the public dissemination of performance criteria and how student performances can be judged in light of those criteria.

What Does "Average" Mean?

Ms. Lafleur teaches mathematics in a middle school in Montreal, Quebec. One unit of instruction during the year involves an introduction to statistics with an emphasis on descriptive statistics. Her goal for all her students is that they will use statistics to describe and predict events in the real world. Last year, Ms. Lafleur had her students design their own research experiments. Teams of four heterogeneously grouped students worked at computer workstations during the unit using a statistical package and graphing software to carry out their work and design a presentation of their findings.

The content she identified as important to teach and assess included several components of statistical problem solving: designing their own research questions, collecting data to answer their questions, representing the variables and data graphically, analyzing their data through statistical methods, interpreting the data they collected, and communicating their understanding through class presentations.

For each of these components she selected examples to illustrate acceptable levels of performance. The previous year she had video-taped students as they presented their statistics projects to the class. She selected examples from these tapes to show different qualities of performance on the components identified. The students were able to gain access to these tapes on their computer screens by choosing a component, as the sample screen (Lavigne 1994) in figure 4 shows.

If the students chose "Data Presentation," for example, they would get a screen that offered access to video examples of both average and above-average performances (see fig. 5). (Although the labels used here were the familiar labels of normative comparison, they were being used to exemplify important performance criteria. They represent "proficient" and "exemplary" levels of performance.) The average example shows a student presenting her group's data as raw scores in a table. In the above-average example, the four students in the group have each made individual pie graphs of different aspects of their data.

In this manner, the students could learn to identify the possible factors that would distinguish an average from an above-average performance for each component of their project.

"In grades 5–8, the mathematics curriculum should include exploration of statistics in real-world situations."
—NCTM (1989, p. 105)

Openness Standard: This assessment provides students with access to samples of other students' work and performance criteria.

Monitoring involves examining evidence at different times.

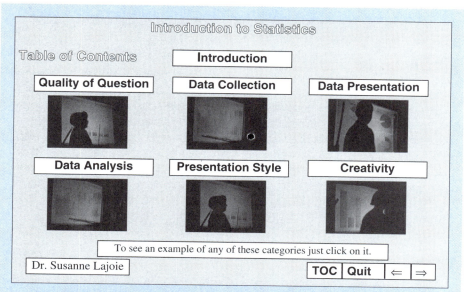

Fig. 4. Table of contents screen (Lavigne 1994)

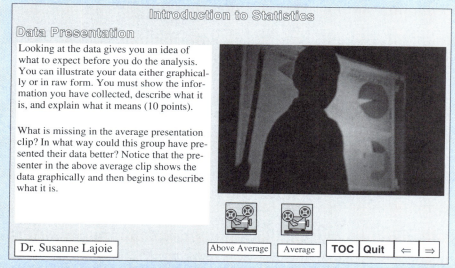

Fig. 5. Data Presentation screen showing video example icons (Lavigne 1994)

Ms. Lafleur also used the computer to store and track evidence of an individual student's progress over time by monitoring each student's use of the computer for graphing and analyzing data. For example, to examine Sabrina's performance, Ms. Lafleur typed her notes on Sabrina into the computer. She noted Sabrina's growth in her ability to organize data. She used a computer program that recorded every action Sabrina took with the computer. She could reexamine these observations whenever she was interested in monitoring a certain component of student growth. In the first week Sabrina had difficulty organizing her data for subsequent analysis, but by the end of the month she was very proficient. Ms. Lafleur added to this computer information other assessment evidence: classroom observations, products of Sabrina's work, Sabrina's responses to quizzes, and her responses to questions about her work that were provided in a written journal. All this evidence was stored in a com-

Inferences Standard: Using multiple sources of evidence can improve the validity of the inferences made about students' learning.

puter database for easy access; it was also used to build a case for Sabrina's progress in statistical problem solving.

This example (adapted from Lajoie et al. [forthcoming]) illustrates the importance of setting high expectations and monitoring the progress of all students if specific goals in mathematical learning are to be accomplished. Note that the computer can store observations, but it is the teacher who must interpret such evidence in order to understand and document students' progress over time. Although the goals for all the students (making sense of a batch of data and being able to communicate findings to others using statistics) contained many components, judgments of progress could be made by both the teacher and the students through continual and recursive monitoring.

COMMUNICATING WITH STUDENTS ABOUT THEIR PERFORMANCE

Communicating with students about their performance is part of a shift toward viewing students as active participants in assessment.

Monitoring students' progress effectively depends on good communication between teachers and students. This communication works in both directions: Teachers gather evidence about students' learning, and then provide feedback to students about their progress. When gathering evidence, teachers can make use of much more than occasional paper-and-pencil tasks.

Example: Listening to Students

One of the most powerful sources of evidence about students' learning comes from listening to students explain their thinking during classroom instruction. In the next example (adapted from Carpenter and Fennema [1992]), a first-grade teacher listens to her students describe alternative strategies for solving problems.

Equity Standard: This teacher encourages multiple paths to the solution of a problem.

How Many Peanuts?

Ms. Morris's first-grade students are solving whole-number addition and subtraction problems. Rather than relying on written tests or formal assessment procedures, Ms. Morris continually asks her students to describe the processes they used to solve a given problem, and students are encouraged to describe alternative solutions. In the following dialogue, the students solve a comparison problem:

Ms. Morris: The African elephant ate 37 peanuts. The Indian elephant ate 43 peanuts. How many fewer peanuts did the African elephant eat than the Indian elephant?

The children worked on the problem for two or three minutes. Some of the children used stacking cubes that had been joined together in stacks of ten cubes. Others did not use any materials. After a minute or so, several of the children raised their hands. After two minutes, only one child, Mike, was still working on the problem. Ms. Morris asked him if he was done. When he shook his head, she told him to keep working. After another thirty seconds, he raised his hand.

Ms. M.: OK? How many fewer peanuts did the African elephant eat? Mike?

Mike: 6.

Ms. M.: Does everyone agree with that?
... How did you figure it out, Mike?

Mike: Well, I had 43 here *(pushing out four stacks of ten cubes and three additional cubes joined together)*, and I had 37 here *(pushing out three stacks of ten cubes and a stack of seven)*. I put 30 on top of these 30. I took 3, and I put them here; there were 4 left, so I took 4 off, and there were 6 left.

As he described what he did, he took three of the ten stacks from the collection of 43 and put them on top of the three ten-stacks in the collection of 37. Then he took the three single cubes from the original set of 43 and put them on top of the seven cubes in the set of 37. Then he took the remaining stack of ten cubes from the original 43 and broke off four cubes. He put these four cubes on the four cubes in the set of 37 that were not covered. He was left with six cubes from the set of 43 that did not match up with cubes in the set of 37.

Used with permission from the Wisconsin Center for Education Research, School of Education, University of Wisconsin—Madison

Ms. M.: What do you think of Mike's solution? ... Did anyone do it a different way?

Marci: I took 37, and I needed 43. So I counted up 3 more. That was 40. Then I took 3 more to 43.

Ms. M.: Good. Does her way work out well? ... It sure does. Did anybody do it differently?

Linda: Well, first I got 37. Then I got 43 *(pushes out collections of 37 and 43 cubes joined together in stacks of ten, with the extra cubes also connected together)*. See, I know it couldn't be 10, because if you had 10, it would be 47 instead of 43. So I realized that it had to be less than 10. So what I did was I imagined 3 more cubes here *(points to the top of the stack of seven cubes in the set of 37)*, and I imagined 3 more right here *(pointing to a space next to the collection of 37 that corresponds to where the three cubes are in the collection of 43)*.

Ms. Morris gave each child in the group time to complete the problems, and she gave children who had a different solution an opportunity to explain their solutions. The children all listened attentively to other children's solutions, so they had the chance to learn from one another. Ms. Morris also learned what each child could do, and she learned more than whether a child got the correct answer. The different solution strategies reflected quite different levels of understanding. Mike had to model the problem directly, whereas the solutions of Marci and Linda showed more flexibility in operating with numbers. While the children were working on the problem, Ms. Morris made notes about the solution processes she observed. These notes helped her in monitoring the students' progress.

Learning Standard: Talking about solutions helps students become better problem solvers.

This example could be extended to reflect growth or change with respect to Mike's ability to solve such comparison problems. His initial strategy, direct modeling with cubes, may be replaced with counting strategies such as Linda's, by writing a sentence (e.g., $37 + \square = 43$) and "counting on from smaller" to find the answer, and so forth. Monitoring Mike's progress in learning to solve a variety of addition and subtraction problems would involve tracking the strategies and procedures he uses to solve such problems over an extended period of time.

Openness Standard: Communicating with students about their progress helps them understand expectations.

Setting goals and gathering evidence of a student's progress in achieving them are unproductive if judgments by teachers or others of his or her performance are not regularly communicated to the student. Students need to understand clearly what is expected; whether their work is of acceptable quality (e.g., the assessment is based on the reasons they give and strategies they use as well as on whether their answers are correct or not); and the effectiveness of the draft, feedback, and revision cycle for the production of large pieces of work. For assessment to be equitable and valid, each student must receive feedback over time on multiple occasions and in multiple formats on tasks that address the breadth of important mathematical content. To satisfy the Coherence Standard, feedback must be part of an assessment system that gives students consistent messages about what mathematics is valued and legitimate ways to demonstrate that knowledge.

The best feedback is descriptive, specific, relevant, timely, and encouraging. It is immediately usable. The feedback may be oral or written, formal or informal, private or public, geared toward an individual or a group. The focus of feedback may be a single assessment activity or multiple activities. Providing effective feedback in a continual and recursive manner will help each student become an independent learner.

Openness Standard: This teacher promptly provides useful information to this student about the quality of his work.

Example: Providing Written Feedback on Students' Work

In this example, a seventh-grade teacher provides feedback intended to help a student interpret his own work according to specific criteria. The teacher allowed his students time in class to explore, working with pattern blocks, the different ways to increase the size of squares, triangles, and trapezoids. After several days of working with the blocks, students were asked to formulate and write down what they had learned.

Stewart's Work

Stewart summarized his work in a diagram and statement (see fig. 6).

Stewart

all squared numbers are the sum of odd numbers because of the picture I made of squared numbers.

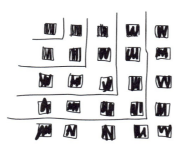

I got the next squared number from 1 by adding 1 and 3 which are odd. Then you add the next odd number 5 and you get the next squared number 9. See how the pattern goes. 16 = 1 + 3 + 5 + 7. Every square will work like that.

Fig. 6. Stewart's work (contributed by Ruth Cossey, Mills College)

Stewart has clearly identified a pattern of squared numbers but has not expressed his conjecture, "All squared numbers are the sum of odd numbers," precisely. The teacher wrote the following note to Stewart and placed it on his report:

Stewart, your work indicates that you know special odd numbers that sum to 16, 1 + 3 + 5 + 7, not just any odd numbers (e.g., 11 + 5). You need to be more convincing that your pattern will always work.

Such feedback helps the student learn that generalizations apply to broad mathematical concepts that may be abstracted from patterns. This feedback also communicated the levels of thinking and completeness of explanations that were expected of Stewart. What would you have said to Stewart about his progress toward making and explaining his mathematical conjectures? What suggestions would you give him to encourage his progress?

Learning Standard: Explicit feedback about performance not only helps students understand what they know and can do but also helps ascertain what they have yet to learn.

Inferences Standard: Teachers use cumulative knowledge about students when giving feedback on individual tasks.

It is possible that your answer to the last two questions is that you do not have enough information. Teachers can make some inferences based on a single activity if they can place it within a context of ongoing performances, but students are better served if most feedback is cumulative and based on many performances.

PERFORMANCE TASKS, PROJECTS, AND PORTFOLIOS AS ASSESSMENT TOOLS

To demonstrate real growth in mathematical power, students need to demonstrate their ability to do major pieces of work that are more elaborate and time-consuming than just short exercises, sets of word problems, and chapter tests. Performance tasks, projects, and portfolios are some examples of more complex instructional and assessment activities. The earlier example of designing an experiment in statistics in Ms. Lafleur's eighth-grade class illustrates the use of *projects* for assessment purposes.

Large pieces of work, like performance tasks, projects, and portfolios, provide opportunities for students to demonstrate growth in mathematical power.

Still another useful assessment tool is a student *portfolio.* During a school year or course (or even several years or courses), each student produces a large amount of work. This material may be kept in a working folder. A portfolio is created by selecting examples from that folder to demonstrate the quality of that student's work in mathematics. The process by which students select what they consider to be their best work is an important means by which they learn to reflect on their own work.

One criterion that teachers take into consideration when designing an assessment is whether a specific activity allows students equal opportunities to demonstrate their knowledge. In fact, one issue teachers face in monitoring student progress is whether the performance tasks they use to judge progress are equitable. Is there a sufficient variety of tasks and do the conditions of the tasks allow students to demonstrate what they know and are able to do?

Example: Judging Progress Equitably

The following example illustrates how a teacher worked with her colleagues to create a geometry assessment task that was also a learning opportunity that gave all students a way to demonstrate their knowledge.

"In grades 9–12, the mathematics curriculum should include numerous and varied experiences that reinforce and extend logical reasoning skills."
—NCTM (1989, p. 143)

Letting Everyone In

At the end of an analytic geometry unit in tenth grade, three teachers, Ms. Lee, Mr. Jackson, and Ms. Romario, were deciding on an assessment task that focused on—

◆ making and testing conjectures;

◆ deducing properties of geometric figures using concepts of functions;

◆ translating between geometric and functional representations;

◆ using dynamic geometry software appropriately.

They decided that the most appropriate assessment would be an investigation similar to one those students had done during the unit. They would have students use the dynamic geometry software they had been using during the unit to investigate a new situation. They wanted the assessment to furnish evidence of what students had learned from exploring geometric situations and making conjectures. Students would continue their learning while doing the assessment.

Ms. Lee suggested the following task as one that might fit these conditions; she argued that it was open ended, yet by focusing on the sum of the distances of various points from a triangle's sides, it required that students work in a geometric function context:

On your computer make a sketch of a triangle ABC, with an interior point D and the shortest segments from D to each of the triangle's sides. To answer the following questions, consider your sketch on the computer.

What conjecture(s) can you make about the sum of the distances from D to the triangle's sides? Do you think your conjecture will apply to any triangle? Make a convincing argument for your answers to these questions. Support your arguments with data you have collected. Use tables or graphs to present your data.

Mr. Jackson commented that he liked the general direction of the task but was concerned that it was *too* open, that students might not get to the rich mathematics that it was possible to explore in the problem. He thought it likely, in fact, that many students would not see much in this context beyond a relationship between the sum of the distances and the triangle's largest and smallest altitudes. He argued for providing more mathematical guidance up front—to increase access, to point in several mathematical directions, to preserve choice. Mr. Jackson revised Ms. Lee's task accordingly:

Take an acute triangle with an interior point P. Consider the perpendiculars from point P to the sides and the triangle formed by the three feet of these perpendiculars on the three sides. This is the pedal triangle of pedal point P. [See fig. 7.]

1) Measure

  a. The sum of the perpendicular distances to the three sides of the original triangle from P.

  b. The sum of the distances from P to the three vertices of the original triangle.

  c. The area of the pedal triangle.

  d. The perimeter of the pedal triangle.

2) Explore how these measures change for different locations of P inside the triangle.

3) What conjectures can you make about the sums, areas, and perimeters found in your explorations? Do you think your conjecture will apply to any triangle?

Learning Standard: How does the assessment engage students in relevant, purposeful work on worthwhile mathematical activities?

Mathematics Standard: Is the mathematics significant?

"For some students, the issue in mathematics is not the learning of mathematical topics and procedures but rather the ability to produce solutions."

—Maria Marolda and Patricia Davidson (1994, p. 97)

- *Make a convincing argument for your answers. Your argument can be written or oral.*

- *Support your argument with the data you collected.*

- *Use tables or graphs to present your data.*

- *Explain a situation where someone would want to know this information.*

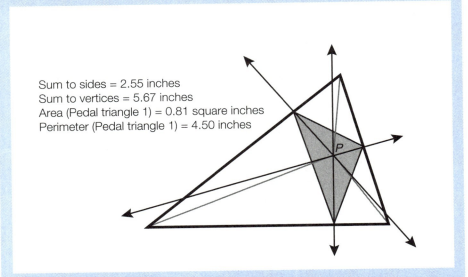

Sum to sides = 2.55 inches
Sum to vertices = 5.67 inches
Area (Pedal triangle 1) = 0.81 square inches
Perimeter (Pedal triangle 1) = 4.50 inches

Fig. 7. An acute triangle with an interior point P

There was general agreement that this task would increase access, but Ms. Romario raised another equity issue: whether the criteria for "make a convincing argument" and whether the term *conjecture* were well understood by the students. It was true that all their students had been exploring geometric situations and discussing their findings, but how carefully had they been monitoring the quality of arguments or the phrasing of conjectures?

Ms. Romario proposed that they first engage the students in an activity before giving Mr. Jackson's revised task as part of an end-of-unit assessment, and then reconvene to discuss their observations. The others agreed and selected an observation task for equilateral triangles as a special case of Mr. Jackson's task (see fig. 8). They would carefully observe the students, listen, give feedback, then reconvene to discuss their data on access and on the students' understanding of the criteria. On that basis, they could elect to give their end-of-unit assessment, modify their criteria, or do some further instruction.

In their subsequent meeting, the teachers pooled their observations—especially regarding students' understanding of the criteria and access to the mathematics represented in the task. Each thought the feedback on the criteria was satisfactory. The teachers also expressed confidence about access: There appeared to be widespread facility with the use of the software; the investigations facilitated the use of supporting conjectures; and the choice between written

"Assessment must provide opportunities for teachers or evaluators ... to determine the students' effectiveness in dealing with the inherent demands of the mathematical topics themselves."
—Maria Marolda and Patricia Davidson (1994, p. 86)

and oral presentations allowed students sufficient latitude. Still, they recognized that there was a potential difficulty for students for whom English was not a first language. In order to address this inequity, students could be given the task in their native language. In addition, they could be given opportunities to respond in the language in which they felt most confident and be encouraged to use multiple methods to communicate. Alternatively, these students could be given more teacher support in English to verify their understanding of the task and to clarify the meaning of their conjectures.

Equity Standard: Does the assessment help students demonstrate their best work?

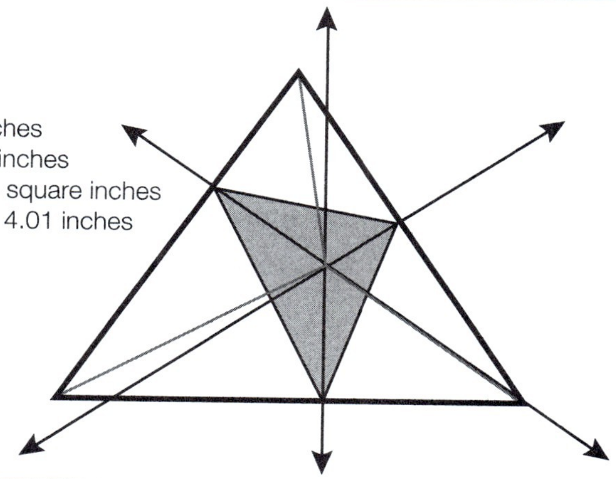

Sum to sides = 2.30 inches
Sum to vertices = 4.63 inches
Area (Polygon 1) = 0.74 square inches
Perimeter (Polygon 1) = 4.01 inches

Fig. 8. An equilateral triangle with an interior point P

This example describes how teachers handled one equity concern, access—that is, whether there were adequate provisions for allowing each student to exhibit his or her best work. For this to occur, each student must understand the task and be sufficiently familiar with its contexts and implicit assumptions to be able to apply and communicate his or her mathematical responses. Such concern about the challenges to the students posed by chosen tasks allows teachers to feel more confident that they are making valid inferences about their students' progress.

Equity Standard: Do the modes of response invite each student to engage in the mathematics?

STUDENTS CAN LEARN TO ASSESS THEIR OWN WORK

Students learn to share responsibility for the assessment process as they come to understand and make judgments about the quality of their own work. The shift in teaching toward helping students increase their capacity for analysis and their ability to formulate problems and communicate correct mathematical work is supported when students become adept at judging the quality of their own work and that of others, as when, for example, selecting work to be included in portfolios. Students also learn to look for ways in which the complex mathematical situations they explore can provide information that will help them determine whether their solution path is reasonable in comparison to other possible strategies they may choose.

Example: Learning to Judge One's Own Work

The following vignette explores the place of self-assessment and peer review in the learning process. Ms. Harris, a fourth-grade teacher, attempted to structure an assessment environment in which students believed they were responsible for one another's learning—that is, they had a right to receive assistance and an obligation to give help when asked.

Mirror Images

Ms. Harris presented this problem to the class: Find a way to figure the area of *any* triangle if you know its height and width.

The homework assignment was to write a report and to critique their own work. Rya remembered using geoboards the previous week to find area. Turning to Cam, her partner, she said, "Before, we used geoboards to find areas of all sorts of weird shapes. Do you think we can use them now?"

Cam looked at the attempts he had made at drawing some triangles on his paper and said, "Ms. Harris said we could use anything we thought might help us solve the problem, so let's try using them. They're fun, anyway."

"It will be easier to make lots of triangles," responded Rya, as she got out the geoboards.

"Yeah, and it's easier to see what their areas are because of the pegs," Cam added.

Cam cleared the rubber bands off his geoboard. Rya grabbed a red rubber band and built a right triangle with a base of 2 units and a height of 2 units on her geoboard. "Look, if you count the little pieces, the area of this triangle is 2 squares." Cam concurred.

They investigated many other triangles and began to make a chart of the height, base, sides, and area of the triangles they built on their geoboards. They noticed that the areas of the right triangles they built were half the area of a rectangle with the same base and height. They came to the conclusion that they could multiply base and height and divide by 2. Obtuse triangles caused them to question their visual representation of doubling the area, but they eventually generalized their formula to include those triangles, too.

The next day, Rya and Cam got together to discuss how to fill out their "self-assessment" sheets.

The class, like every fourth-grade class in the state, was using specific criteria to assess mathematical reasoning and communication (Petit 1992). Part of the sheet that Rya and Cam were working on is shown in figure 9.

Sitting cross-legged on the gray rug surrounded by benches, Cam and Rya exchanged papers. Ms. Harris, who had not talked with them as they worked on their investigation, decided to listen in on the conversation.

"How did we get that formula?" inquired Cam.

Vermont Mathematics Criteria

Student Self-Assessment

PS 1: Understanding the Task

1	2	3	4
I didn't understand enough to get started or even make progress.	I understood enough to solve part of the problem or get part of a solution.	I understood the problem.	I identified special factors that influenced the way I approached the problem.

PS 2: How You Solved the Problem

1	2	3	4
My approach didn't work.	My approach would only let me solve part of the problem.	My approach would work for the problem.	My approach was efficient or sophisticated.

PS 3: Why—Decisions along the Way

1	2	3	4
I had no reasons for the decisions I made.	I knew I was reasoning but it's hard to see from my work.	Although I didn't clearly explain the reasons for my decisions, my work suggests reasoning was used.	I clearly exhibited reasons for the decisions I made along the way.

PS 4: So What—Outcomes of Activities

1	2	3	4
I solved the problem and then stopped.	I solved the problem and then made comments about something I observed in my solution.	I solved the problem and connected my solution to other math that I knew or I described a use for what I learned in the "real world."	After I solved the problem, I made a general rule about the solution or I extended the solution to a more complicated situation.

C 1: Mathematical Language

1	2	3	4

Fig. 9. Vermont mathematics criteria (adapted from Petit 1992, p. 15, and used with permission)

"Well, Cam ... what did we do? ... Oh, yeah, we saw that there were two triangles in the rectangle."

"You didn't put that in your write-up (see fig. 10). Remember, Ms. Harris wants to know why we came up with our answers."

"Right, that's what she means by explaining our decisions? OK, I'll say why you get the area if you multiply and then divide by 2. I think I'm done."

Rya started to get up to leave, but Cam continued to question her.

"Last night I decided not to put *side* in my chart. I never used it for an area. I wasn't even sure what it meant."

Rya got on all fours to explain. "Well, it's not the height, and it's not the length, it's, you know, the other side."

"Oh, yeah! But look, I don't think *this* slanty side of the triangle is only one unit long."

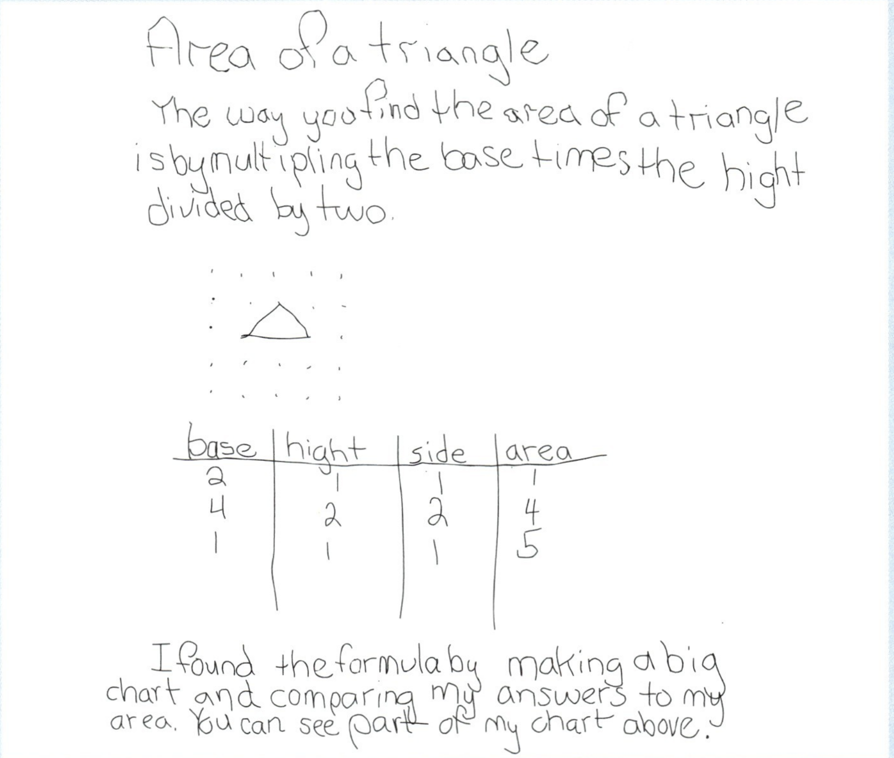

Area of a triangle

The way you find the area of a triangle is by multipling the base times the hight divided by two.

base	hight	side	area
2	1	1	1
4	2	2	4
1	1	1	5

I found the formula by making a big chart and comparing my answers to my area. You can see part of my chart above.

Fig. 10. Rya's report (contributed by Clare Forseth, Marion Cross Schools)

"You don't think so? Here, give me my paper. Let's see. Oh, you may be right. If I swing that side so it's straight up and down, it would go above the peg."

Cam further convinced himself that they had made a mistake about the length of the hypotenuse of the right triangles they had sketched. "And do you see that slant line is also a diagonal of that little square, so it has to be longer than the side of the square."

"I see what you mean. Since we didn't use it in our formula, maybe we should just get rid of that column in our reports." Glancing at Cam's report (see fig. 11), Rya noticed the diagrams. "Oooh! You have lots of pictures of triangles in your report. That's a good idea, 'cause that way the drawings help you explain and you don't have to write so much. I'm going to add more pictures to mine. Oh, and I like the way you labeled your triangles, but I think that's not how you spell *obtuse*."

The next day as Rya read over her revised solution, she thought to herself, "I bet this is my best piece so far." She scanned the criteria sheet. She felt more confident in assessing herself now. Cam had helped her see how to explain her reasoning more clearly.

Ms. Harris noted that Cam used his pictures as models when he explained the diagonal lines. Rya seemed to be moving beyond a just-get-something-down approach to really wanting to learn and to share her thinking in a way others would understand. Ms. Harris was happy

Learning Standard: Self-assessment provides a valuable learning opportunity.

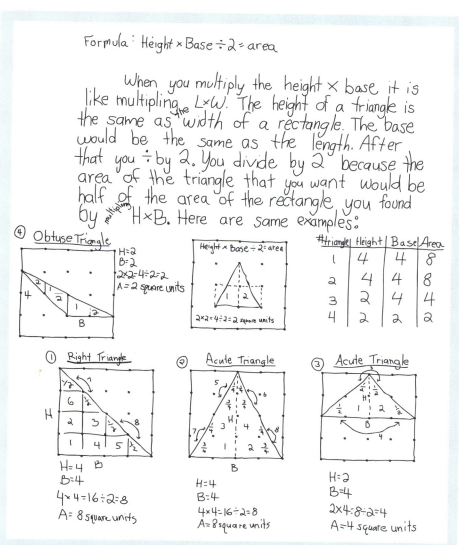

Formula: Height × Base ÷ 2 = area

When you multiply the height × base it is like multipling the LxW. The height of a triangle is the same as the width of a rectangle. The base would be the same as the length. After that you ÷ by 2. You divide by 2 because the area of the triangle that you want would be half of the area of the rectangle you found by multiplying H×B. Here are same examples:

Fig. 11. Cam's report (contributed by Clare Forseth, Marion Cross Schools)

to see that their discussions and reports had moved beyond simply noting a procedure to include justifications for their approaches. The students knew that she would use the same assessment sheet to give them feedback on their finished product. She thought that this time her assessment and theirs would be pretty close, which would be another indication that the students were beginning to understand the quality of their work and would be in a good position to select the best pieces of work for their portfolios.

Students in this vignette were being encouraged to monitor themselves and their peers. By providing opportunities for students to evaluate, reflect on, and improve their own work, teachers help students become independent learners.

Inferences Standard: When students learn to assess themselves, they become independent learners.

SUMMARY

Monitoring students' progress in classrooms enhances each student's learning to the extent that it facilitates and encourages continued learning and helps each student become an independent learner. Effective monitoring of students' progress requires clarity about—

♦ the mathematics to be learned;

♦ the kinds of evidence necessary to describe students' progress in learning that mathematics;

♦ the variety of equitable assessment methods and tools available to collect evidence of students' learning;

♦ the criteria for interpreting that evidence and making valid inferences about what students are learning;

♦ how those interpretations are to be communicated to students in ways that support the achievement of instructional goals.

Well-planned monitoring of students' progress provides meaningful information to both teachers and learners. Continual and comprehensive monitoring allows teachers to make more informed decisions about students' growth in mathematical power. Students who are clear about their learning goals and the progress they are making toward them are more likely to be reflective and confident learners of mathematics.

PURPOSE: MAKING INSTRUCTIONAL DECISIONS

When teachers have a good understanding of what their students know and can do, they are able to make appropriate instructional decisions. Such decisions may include identifying appropriate content, sequencing and pacing lessons, modifying or extending activities for students' particular needs, and choosing effective methodologies and representations. The NCTM *Professional Standards for Teaching Mathematics* emphasized the role of assessment in providing the information needed for analyzing teaching and learning and asserted that "assessment of students and analysis of instruction are fundamentally interconnected" (p. 63). The primary question to be answered in using assessment to make instructional decisions is, "How can I use evidence about my students' progress to make instructional decisions?"

The process of using assessment to make instructional decisions involves using evidence of learning from the students in the classroom. Evidence is used in three ways: (1) to examine the effects of the tasks, discourse, and learning environment on students' mathematical knowledge, skills, and dispositions; (2) to make instruction more responsive to students' needs; and (3) to ensure that every student is gaining mathematical power. Although evidence of progress originates with individual students, as indicated in the "Purpose: Monitoring Students' Progress" section, teachers also sample and collect such evidence to provide information about the progress of the groups of students they teach. They make instructional decisions and adapt their teaching to respond simultaneously to the needs of individuals and of groups. The quality of teachers' instructional decisions depends, in part, on the quality of their assessment and their purposeful sampling of evidence during instruction. When teachers use appropriate evidence of what their students understand and can do in making instructional decisions, their teaching responds to individual and group needs.

The Assessment Standards suggest shifts in assessment practices to support more responsive instructional decisions. These include shifts—

♦ toward integrating assessment with instruction (to provide data for moment-by-moment instructional decisions) and away from depending on scheduled testing (generally useful only for delayed instructional decisions);

♦ toward using evidence from a variety of assessment formats and contexts for determining the effectiveness of instruction and away from relying on any one source of information (often, in the past, paper-and-pencil tests);

♦ toward using evidence of every student's progress toward long-range goals in instructional planning and away from planning for content coverage with little regard for students' progress.

"The teacher of mathematics should engage in ongoing analysis of teaching and learning by—

♦ *observing, listening to, and gathering other information about students to assess what they are learning;*

♦ *examining effects of the tasks, discourse, and learning environment on students' mathematical knowledge, skills, and dispositions ..."*
—*NCTM (1991, p. 63)*

INTEGRATING ASSESSMENT WITH INSTRUCTION: MOMENT-BY-MOMENT DECISIONS

Observing, questioning, and listening are the primary sources of evidence for assessment that is continual, recursive, and integrated with instruction.

Integrating assessment and instruction in the classroom means precisely that: assessing students' learning to inform teachers as they make moment-by-moment instructional decisions about students' work in the classroom. Such a blurring of the boundary between instruction and assessment is consistent with the Learning Standard, which presents assessment as an *opportunity* for learning rather than an interruption in the learning process. Observing, listening, and questioning are the most common methods for gathering evidence of learning during instruction.

"The teacher has a central role in orchestrating oral and written discourse in ways that contribute to students' understanding of mathematics."

—NCTM (1991, p. 35)

Posing appropriate questions to students is important for moment-by-moment assessment so that the progress of the group can be monitored and used in planning and teaching. Careful questioning and probing are often needed to determine what students are thinking during a lesson. *Professional Standards for Teaching Mathematics* provides a list of useful suggestions for questioning and talking with students (pp. 3–4). Teachers can learn to be perceptive in interpreting student talk, to make quick decisions about the flow of discourse, and to adapt their instruction appropriately.

The six Assessment Standards furnish a framework for helping teachers monitor their instruction and assessment practices as they gather evidence during instruction. Each standard could be interpreted with questions like the following:

♦ How does the mathematics of the lesson fit within a framework of overall goals for learning important mathematics?

♦ How do these activities contribute to students' learning of mathematics and my understanding of what they are learning?

♦ What opportunity does each student have to engage in these activities and demonstrate what he or she knows and can do?

♦ How are students familiarized with the purposes and goals of the activities, the criteria for determining quality in the achievement of those goals, and the consequences of their performances?

♦ How are multiple sources of evidence used for making valid inferences that lead to helpful decisions?

♦ How do the assessment and instructional content and processes match broader curricular and educational goals?

Questioning a few students often leads to a redirection of the lesson for all. The justification for changing the direction of a lesson could come from the confusion ensuing as third graders attempt to measure their heights with metersticks or from the excited conversation of high school juniors exploring exponential functions on a graphing calculator. Similarly, a teacher might adjust plans for the week as a result of recognizing that students' responses to a problem are far richer than expected, musing, "Terrific! I hadn't thought of so many ways to do this problem. I wonder if there are even more. Maybe we should spend some more time on it tomorrow."

Example: Changing Plans in Mid-Lesson

The vignette that follows illustrates how the interactive nature of assessment and instruction in the classroom can enhance learning. In this story, a sixth-grade student made the incorrect conjecture that all shapes with equal perimeters have equal areas. His teacher decided the misconception was worth exploring in class and changed her lesson plan accordingly.

Inside, Out, and All About

Janna McKnight perched on the edge of her desk at the back of the classroom. Her sixth-grade students were elbowing each other and chatting while parading to the front of the room to place their yellow stickies on a bar chart. They had been finding the area of a salt marsh on a map, a rather irregular shape. Each stickie represented the area (in thousands of square meters) determined by one student.

Mathematics Standard: Encouraging students to make conjectures and seek verification involves them in doing significant mathematics.

The portion of the chart from about 85 to 95 was beginning to look like the New York City skyline, with high-rise towers huddled close together. Close in, to the left and right of the city, were several lower towers. Off to the right at 196 was one lonely stickie with the initials TP, and down to the left were two other stickies at 55 with the initials BT and AK.

Ms. McKnight called the class to order. "All right, let's see what you've found. Who'd like to make some observations about our data?"

Used with permission from the Wisconsin Center for Education Research, School of Education, University of Wisconsin—Madison

"Ninety-two thousand square meters got the most, but 87 was a close second," Jeremy answered. "It seems like lots of people got answers between 86 and 94."

"The lowest answer was 55—two people got that—and the highest was 196. Those people must have done it wrong, because those answers are, like, too different to be true," Angel offered.

"Bernice, is the 55 with BT on it yours?" Wallace blurted.

"The 196 is mine, and it isn't wrong!" Tyler offered in a defensive tone.

Anthony interrupted. "Bernice and I worked together, but I think our calculator gave us the wrong answer. I just added it up again, and ours should be 85 instead of 55."

"Tyler, would you like to explain how you found 196 as the area of the marsh?"

"Well, you remember how we put string around those circles the other day? You didn't give us any string today. But my sweatshirt has

Students should make connections between area and perimeter in meaningful contexts instead of learning those topics as isolated, formula-based skills.

Equity Standard: Perceptive questioning helps all students explain what they know and can do.

a string in the hood, so I pulled it out and wrapped it around the marsh. Then I straightened it out into a square on top of the plastic, and it was about 14 units long and 14 wide. So its area was about 196. The square wasn't exactly 14, but it was pretty close!"

"So, Tyler found the area of a square he built from reshaping a string that fit around the perimeter of the marsh. I noticed most of the rest of you doing something quite different. Amy?"

Amy explained that her group had put clear plastic graph paper on top of the marsh and counted squares. Dyanne explained how her group counted partial squares as halves or fourths for more accuracy.

"Did anyone approach the problem differently? What do you think about Tyler's procedure?"

"I think it's a lot better," said Richard, "because Tyler didn't have to do all that counting. I wish I'd thought of making it into an easier shape. It would have saved a lot of work."

"But why is Tyler's answer so much bigger?" asked Nancy. "I don't know why it's wrong, but Tyler's answer is way too big."

"If the distance around the marsh is a lot, then the area is a lot—wouldn't that be right? Like when one is big, the other is big?" asked Cindy. Numerous heads nodded in agreement, amid a few dissenting frowns.

Pointing to the bulletin board, where dot-paper records of a geoboard activity from the previous week were displayed, Dyanne reminded the class that shapes with equal perimeters could have very different areas.

"All right," said Ms. McKnight, glancing at the clock over the chalkboard. "We're not going to have time today to get to the bottom of this mystery. Let's just write Tyler's conjecture on the board and see whether we can investigate it further tomorrow. Who can use some good mathematical language to say what Tyler's been thinking?"

Inferences Standard: Careful questioning and probing provide evidence for making valid inferences about students' understanding.

Learning Standard: Together, assessment and instruction can build on students' understanding, interests, and experiences.

Janna McKnight wisely did not dismiss Tyler's answer as wrong but probed to discover the source of his confusion. In doing so, she uncovered a common misconception about area and perimeter and made some decisions to adjust her instruction.

What will Ms. McKnight do tomorrow in class? The decisions that she made today have led her to a point where she will have to revise her short-range plans for tomorrow's lesson. She will need to think about ways to follow up on Tyler's conjecture. One of her goals now is to help her students explore the conjecture and decide its validity for themselves, so she wants to plan an activity to make that happen. One idea would be to have them measure the area and perimeter of their own handprints (with fingers spread and with fingers together) and explore the relationship, hoping they will begin to understand why Tyler's conjecture is false. This short-range plan also fits some of her long-range goals for the class. She wants her students to have a sense of what it really means to do mathematics, and she intends to communicate the principle that making conjectures and testing them for validity are important components of mathematical power.

Janna McKnight's understanding of the importance of conjecture and verification in doing mathematics helps her recognize the value of exploring Tyler's conjecture rather than quickly pointing out his error. Teachers are more effective in assessing students' understanding of mathematical ideas when they are knowledgeable about performance standards, familiar with the "big ideas" of mathematics (such as number sense, proportion, and equivalence), confident of their abilities to deal with important mathematical processes (such as problem solving, reasoning, communication, and making connections), and convinced of the importance of dispositions (such as motivation and confidence). Ongoing professional development activities—attending conferences, reading professional journals, and collaborating with other educators—help teachers become aware of, and confident in, their understanding of effective ways to help all students become mathematically powerful.

"It is students' acts of construction and invention that build their mathematical power and enable them to solve problems they have never seen before."
—Mathematical Sciences Education Board (1989, p. 59)

USING MULTIPLE SOURCES OF EVIDENCE FOR SHORT-TERM PLANNING

In making short-range plans, teachers use assessment evidence to make decisions about tomorrow, the day after, and next week. As they plan a unit of instruction, they review their goals and long-range plans and reconsider those plans in light of information they have gathered about their students' learning. As teachers consciously try to integrate instruction and assessment, they identify places in the unit at which they will check for specific types of understanding, or ask certain questions, or collect certain work to inform themselves as they make instructional decisions.

Short-term instructional decisions are improved when teachers are informed by evidence from observations, questioning, and students' products. This evidence provides views of learning at varying levels of complexity that can be compared to performance criteria and expectations. However, a systematic approach to gathering complex data from a variety of formats requires additional planning for the specific data to be gathered. Observations and questioning offer opportunities for understanding the influences of students' unique prior experiences. Unexplained differences in written work may be the result of inequities that become apparent from questioning and observing. Combining documented evidence, from observations and questions, with written products gives a more complete picture of students' mathematical power than can be obtained from tests, quizzes, and assignments that focus primarily on the mastery of procedures.

Equity Standard: Differences in students' work may be better understood through evidence from observations and questioning.

Numerous useful assessment formats—such as journals, portfolios, writing, projects, and extended investigations—require advance planning and extra time to communicate expectations and criteria for scoring to students. Because they are more complex than quick-answer questions on quizzes and tests, these formats can furnish evidence of learning not often captured by simpler formats.

Example: Using Evidence to Plan Tomorrow's Lesson

In the next example, Mr. Ernest uses observation to determine the extent to which his first-grade students are making sense of the important mathematical concepts involved in nonstandard measurement. While planning for subsequent lessons, he reflects on what he has learned about his students' conceptual understandings and how their understandings are reflected in their work.

"It Took 8 Perpl Rods"

Sitting at his desk after school, Charlie Ernest quickly recorded some anecdotal comments about what he had observed during the rod-measuring activity his first graders had done that day with sets of colored rods of various lengths. He paused as he thought about what the class should do tomorrow and how tomorrow's work would fit into his long-range plan. Certainly the children had enjoyed the work today. There had been lots of laughter, especially when Trey tried to measure John's smile with white rods. And Terrance had been triumphant when he and Jenise successfully measured her lunch bag.

Jenise had placed a black rod adjacent to the closed end of her lunch bag and furrowed her brow as she dipped her head to table height, squinting a sightline along the rod to make sure that the rod and bag were even. Terrance had a plan.

Used with permission from the Wisconsin Center for Education Research, School of Education, University of Wisconsin—Madison

"You do one black one, and I'll do one. We'll take turns. Then we can do the purple ones." He had quickly plopped another black rod down, touching the end of Jenise's. She placed a black rod next to his and straightened his out. After placing one more black rod, Terrance lifted his hands. "Four," he shouted, "that'll do it. FOUR! That's all we can do. Write it down!"

Jenise wrote in large neat letters: *We mesured my lunch bag. For the blak one we got 4 and haf becus there was some bag left over. We mesured the longest way.*

Terrance was lining up purple rods while Jenise was writing. "Eight," he said. "It took eight purple rods." Jenise passed the paper to Terrance. "Naw, you write it," he said.

"No, it's your turn," Jenise replied. Terrance never wanted to write. Draw maybe, but write—never. Still, Jenise convinced him that it was his job to continue.

He dashed off this sentence: *It took 8 perpl rods.*

After school, Mr. Ernest thought about what his children were learning about measurement. He had expected that they would use different-colored rods to repeatedly measure the same objects, and he had hoped that he could see evidence that they understood how the size of the unit made a difference in the measurements they obtained. Indeed, most of the students had indicated on their papers what units they were using. Although Sara and Tran had not written down the color of the rods with their measurements, when Mr. Ernest asked them to explain, Tran knew which colors went with which measurements.

What else had Mr. Ernest noted during his observations? Well, he had not anticipated Jenise's use of a fraction. Now he was curious to learn how the other students were dealing with the issue of measurements that were not whole numbers.

It was late. Mr. Ernest reviewed the questions he had written in his plan book for tomorrow's class:

- *Yesterday, Trina measured the side of her table with rods. She said it was about 12 rods long. Did anyone else get a different answer? (Write all answers on the board.)*

- *Discuss with a neighbor why you think we came up with different measures for the length of Trina's desk. (Allow discussion time.) Who would like to report back what you and your partner came up with?*

- *If it takes about 12 blue rods to measure the desk, what color rods would you need more than 12 of? How do you know?*

Mr. Ernest knew the first question would get a set of data on the board and prompt the students to begin questioning the data. As usual, he would get the whole class involved with the problem by asking them to talk with a partner. This would provide more opportunities to listen to and observe his students. He would also probe their thinking further by asking "Why?" and "How did you know?" He was very interested in finding out which students were making sense of the concept that it takes fewer longer rods, and how they would show that understanding as they justified their actions and answers to his questions.

Inferences Standard: Mr. Ernest recognizes the need for multiple sources of evidence in making inferences about his students' understandings of measurement and fractions.

Mr. Ernest considered how he might modify or add to tomorrow's questions as a result of his curiosity about his students' estimation abilities when confronting fractional measurements. Maybe he would ask, "Did anyone measure something that the rod-train didn't fit exactly? What measurement did you report? How did you decide on that number?" And he might start planning a few lessons that would involve his students in an informal exploration of simple fraction concepts.

As this vignette illustrates, assessing students' learning in more complex ways than simply checking for correct answers on written work is a difficult challenge for teachers, a challenge requiring an approach to both teaching and planning instruction that is different from traditional practice. Teachers must choose appropriate activities, pose good questions, listen carefully to students' responses, and follow up with questions that help students communicate what they think and can do. An understanding of how students learn specific mathematical concepts is important, including an awareness of common misconceptions and a familiarity with strategies for helping students describe and reconsider their understandings. Students' potential strategies can be considered and anticipated during short-term planning.

USING EVIDENCE OF LEARNING IN LONG-RANGE PLANNING

In addition to making decisions during instruction and planning for the next day's lesson, teachers plan over longer time spans. Before the start of a new school year, they plan the broad topics with which they will engage their students. These plans are often altered during the course of the school year because evidence that students are developing mathematical power enables teachers to make more informed plans and alterations as the class progresses.

The key to ensuring that every student is learning important mathematics and becoming mathematically powerful is to make valid inferences about each student's learning as it proceeds. Such inferences require a balance of information across a number of dimensions. Therefore, it is important that instructional plans include methods for assessing a broad range of components of mathematical power (e.g., each student's confidence as a mathematics learner, success in solving problems in various contexts, conceptual understandings, and experience in communicating effectively). These varieties of formats, contexts, and occasions must be considered during long-range planning.

Making valid inferences about students' learning requires familiarity with every student's responses in a variety of modes, such as talking, writing, graphing, or illustrating, and in a variety of contexts. When instruction includes group work, then group work needs to be assessed. Cultural considerations are also important; however, care should be taken not to make assumptions based on cultural stereotypes, because each student has unique responses to experiences in and out of school. For non–native speakers of English, encouraging the use of the native language might be appropriate, as well as using English-enhancing preparatory activities. As teachers become familiar with their students—through the careful collection and analysis of relevant assessment data—appropriate instructional decisions can be made.

This is an example of using multiple sources of evidence.

Inferences Standard: Valid inferences require that opportunities be provided for responses in a variety of modes. Equity can be addressed by English-enhancing preparatory activities such as—

♦ *using pictorial and manipulative materials;*

♦ *distinguishing between the language used in daily communication and the language of mathematics;*

♦ *controlling the range of vocabulary and the use of idiomatic expressions.*

Example: Selecting Appropriate Instructional Experiences

Sometimes long-range plans are open to change. A teacher may have a clear picture of the major mathematical concepts she wants to engage her students in, but as the year progresses she may need more detailed evidence of students' understanding in order to decide which units are appropriate. In the next example a high school teacher uses one particular task to help her decide which of two units to teach.

Postal Patterns

Ms. Naman, an eleventh-grade teacher, planned an assessment activity specifically to help her decide which of two units of study would be more appropriate for her students. In looking over the core curriculum for the eleventh grade, Ms. Naman asked herself whether the units she had already planned would adequately meet the standards on algebraic representations and functions. She was concerned about providing instruction at the appropriate level of difficulty and setting an appropriate pace. Among her goals for her students were two of the Curriculum Standards for grades 9–12. She wanted them to learn to "represent situations that involve variable quantities with expressions, equations, inequalities, and matrices" (NCTM 1989, p. 150) and to "represent and analyze relationships using tables, verbal rules, equations, and graphs" (NCTM 1989, p. 154).

Ms. Naman had eight teaching units available, but from her previous experiences she expected to have time for only seven. Which unit should she omit? Two of the units heavily emphasized statistics, which she believed to be practical as well as motivating material. However, the mathematical modeling unit seemed to furnish more opportunities for students to learn about algebraic representations and functions.

Ms. Naman decided that, depending largely on how well her students could work with equations and graphs, she would choose either the second statistics unit or the mathematical modeling unit. As a result, one item on her assessment agenda early in the year was to get a sense of her students' facility in recognizing and expressing mathematical relationships through algebraic and geometric modeling.

In mid-September, after her students had done some work with patterns and graphing, Ms. Naman presented them with the Postal Rate History assessment task (adapted from Connecticut State Department of Education 1991) shown in figures 12 and 13. Two of her students, Chris and Kelly, produced the work shown.

Quite a few of Ms. Naman's students did work that was similar to Chris's (fig. 12). Chris looked for patterns in the differences between the years and the postage costs. However, perhaps because he did not graph the data, no discernible pattern emerged. Chris then oversimplified the problem by finding the average postage increase per year—in essence assuming that the overall relationship was linear. Using this assumption, he calculated predictions for future costs that were far from realistic.

"In grades 9–12, the mathematics curriculum should include the continued study of algebraic concepts and methods so that all students can—

♦ *represent situations that involve variable quantities with expressions, equations, inequalities, and matrices ..."*

—NCTM (1989, p. 150)

"In grades 9–12, the mathematics curriculum should include the continued study of functions so that all students can represent and analyze relationships using tables, verbal rules, equations, and graphs."

—NCTM (1989, p. 154)

Postal Rate History

Postal rates have been figured by the ounce since July 1, 1885. Here are the rates for the past 62 years:

July 6, 1932	3 cents
Aug. 1, 1958	4 cents
Jan. 7, 1963	5 cents
Jan. 7, 1968	6 cents
May 16, 1971	8 cents
March 2, 1974	10 cents
Dec. 31, 1975	13 cents
May 29, 1978	15 cents
March 22, 1981	18 cents
Nov. 1, 1981	20 cents
Feb. 17, 1985	22 cents
April 3, 1988	25 cents
Feb. 3, 1991	29 cents

Based on the postal rates since 1932:
• Predict the cost of mailing a one ounce first class letter in 2001.
• When, if ever, do you think the cost will be 50 cents? $1.00?
Explain your reasoning.

The mailing cost in 2001 will be $.36 or $.37. I think this because over the past 62 years the price has gone up 11 times at an average of 2.27 cents every 3 years. So I believe if you multiply 2.27 cents by 3.33 (3 into 10) you will get a rise of 7.56 cents. So in 2021 the price will be 50 cents. 2091 it will be $1.00.

Fig. 12. Chris's work (task adapted from Connecticut State Department of Education 1991)

Kelly's solution (fig. 13) was one of the most sophisticated ones produced by the students in Ms. Naman's class. Her graph showed clearly that the overall relationship was nonlinear, although for larger values on her y-scale, it appeared that a line might approximate the curve rather well. In fact, Kelly observed that postal costs increased at almost a constant rate between 1971 and 1991 (about $0.10 every ten years) and used this information to predict future costs. However, Kelly's work showed that she, too, had limited experience with graphing. Her x-scale was inconsistent (30, 50, 70, 90, 92, 94, 96 . . .), and she failed to extend the graph to make estimates of future costs.

Inferences Standard: Inferences about students' mathematical knowledge, understanding, and thinking processes inform teachers as they make decisions to adjust instructional plans.

Ms. Naman used the fact that the typical work of her students was like Chris's as one piece of evidence that her students probably needed more experience with analyzing relationships using tables, equations, and graphs. The fact that even some of the strong responses showed a lack of experience with graphing further supported this view. She decided to teach the mathematical modeling unit rather than try to cover both statistics units. If most students had demonstrated an understanding similar to Kelly's, the second statistics unit might have been more appropriate.

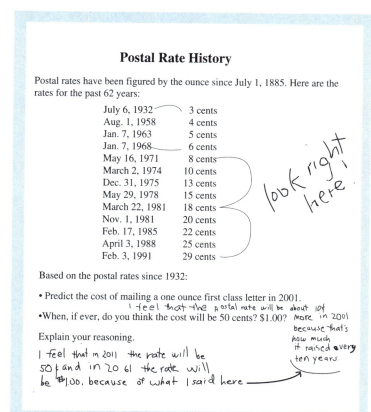

Postal Rate History

Postal rates have been figured by the ounce since July 1, 1885. Here are the rates for the past 62 years:

July 6, 1932	3 cents
Aug. 1, 1958	4 cents
Jan. 7, 1963	5 cents
Jan. 7, 1968	6 cents
May 16, 1971	8 cents
March 2, 1974	10 cents
Dec. 31, 1975	13 cents
May 29, 1978	15 cents
March 22, 1981	18 cents
Nov. 1, 1981	20 cents
Feb. 17, 1985	22 cents
April 3, 1988	25 cents
Feb. 3, 1991	29 cents

look right here!

Based on the postal rates since 1932:

• Predict the cost of mailing a one ounce first class letter in 2001.

I feel that the postal rate will be about 10¢

•When, if ever, do you think the cost will be 50 cents? $1.00?

more in 2001 because that's how much it raised every ten years.

Explain your reasoning.

I feel that in 2011 the rate will be 50¢ and in 2061 the rate will be $1.00, because of what I said here

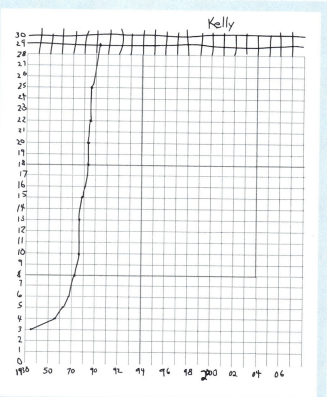

Fig. 13. Kelly's work (task adapted from Connecticut State Department of Education 1991)

SUMMARY

The quality of teachers' instructional decisions is dependent, in large part, on the quality of the assessment that provides information for making those decisions and supports the teachers' analysis of teaching and learning in their classrooms. To ensure that every student become mathematically powerful, effective instruction should be influenced by assessment that focuses on—

♦ the mathematics to be learned;

♦ the variety of evidence available from observations, questioning, and student products;

♦ valid inferences from that evidence;

♦ understanding the diversity of students' learning in the classroom so that the needs of all students are considered.

Many of the goals for improved assessment are achieved through coherent shifts in instructional approaches and assessment strategies. Complex learning activities that engage students in solving nonroutine problems and justifying their strategies and solutions can furnish the needed evidence of learning that teachers rely on to make instructional decisions that are responsive to their students' needs.

PURPOSE: EVALUATING STUDENTS' ACHIEVEMENT

Evaluation is the process of determining worth or assigning a value to something, based on careful examination and judgment.

At regular intervals, students' work is examined, summarized, and reported. Reports thus compiled are designed to indicate each student's mathematical accomplishments at the time. Typically, these formal reports are based on a teacher's judgments about the student's demonstrated understanding or on scores from examinations. Examples are narrative reports of progress, checklists of course criteria achieved, grades on report cards, and scores on comprehensive examinations. The basic question is, How does each student's understanding at this time compare with the goals he or she was expected to have achieved?

Evaluations of students' achievement at particular times have several characteristics. They are summative in nature, are usually designed to communicate to audiences beyond the classroom, and are often used to make important educational decisions for the students (e.g., admission, placement, certification). Because of the importance of such decisions for each student, the *inferences* made from summary evaluations and the way those summaries are created are the focus of this section. However, conscious and careful consideration must be given to the relationship of all six Assessment Standards to the evaluation of students' achievement.

Note that many assessments for the purpose of evaluating students' achievement are closely related to a previous purpose, "Monitoring Students' Progress," in that both deal with information about individual students that is drawn from their work. In fact, much of the same data can be, and often is, used for both purposes. During the course of instruction, teachers monitor each student's progress toward specified mathematical goals and provide feedback that will help each student accomplish those goals. When teachers evaluate a student's achievement, they make judgments about each student's understanding of mathematics at a particular time with respect to the specific knowledge and performance criteria associated with those goals, and they formally summarize and report on the student's progress.

For assessment to be consistent with the reform vision of school mathematics and these Assessment Standards, several shifts in the way student achievement is evaluated are warranted. Four related shifts in practice are of particular importance:

♦ Toward comparing students' performance with performance criteria and away from comparing student with student

♦ Toward assessing students' growth in mathematical power and away from assessing students' knowledge of specific facts and isolated skills

♦ Toward certification based on balanced, multiple sources of information and away from relying on only a few, narrowly conceived sources of evidence about student learning

♦ Toward profiles of achievement based on public criteria and away from single letter grades based on variable or nonpublic criteria

COMPARING STUDENTS' WORK WITH PERFORMANCE CRITERIA

In North America, grading practices have followed certain customs and traditions for many years. Beginning at some point in elementary school and continuing through high school, teachers have reported their evaluations of student work by awarding a letter grade, usually A, B, C, D, or F; writing a number between 1 and 100; or using a scale from unsatisfactory to excellent. There are certain assumptions that the public makes about this practice. One is that, in general, grades are based on the comparison of students with other students, so that the distribution of grades should follow an expected pattern: for example, there should be more Cs than any other grade and fewer As and Fs. However, this assumption is both outdated and counterproductive. Grades do not have to be the result of comparisons among students.

Example: Rethinking the Meaning of Grades

An alternative way to conceive of grades is to measure students' achievement against performance criteria. Using performance criteria as the basis for a student's grade puts the emphasis on the development of each student's mathematical understanding rather than on competition among students.

What Is an A?

The mathematics teachers at Jordan High School tried to counter the belief that grades reflected comparative performance with others by coming to a new agreement on the meanings of each letter grade. When students turned in problems of the week, the teachers decided that they would award a C for a response that was complete but did not go beyond what was expected of all students. A B would be given for solutions that were well presented and that indicated the student had a solid knowledge of the mathematics. The teachers reserved an A for students who formed generalizations or provided some other extension of the problem. These teachers were working on a scoring scale for students' achievement that was consistent with the development of mathematical understanding and problem solving. Higher grades were given to students who demonstrated more complete understanding of the mathematics and communicated that knowledge appropriately.

To make this transition successful, the teachers invited the students to participate in the process of developing the new general scoring rubric. Samples of students' work were examined by the students, followed by discussions of what constituted exemplary work as well as work at other levels. Samples of these "anchor papers" were sent home to parents to inform them of

Grades based on demonstrated depth of mathematical knowledge communicate more about students' developing mathematical understanding than grades based on a student's relative position in the class or on percentage points.

Used with permission from the Wisconsin Center for Education Research, School of Education, University of Wisconsin—Madison

the new system, and parents were encouraged to comment. The teachers discovered that their first attempts at developing the rubric were rough drafts—that is, they had to remain open to constant revision and refinement as new understanding was developed of what each grade meant.

Open assessment involves shared responsibilities by students, teachers, and the public.

ASSESSING GROWTH IN MATHEMATICAL POWER

Mathematics Standard: How does the assessment elicit the use of mathematics that is important to know and be able to do? How does the assessment engage students in realistic and worthwhile mathematical activities?

Another assumption the public makes about traditional grading practices is that grades represent the full range of students' achievement. On the contrary, assessments seldom provide evidence of higher-order thinking skills, and grades often include other factors, such as effort, along with achievement. The Assessment Standards call for a shift away from assessment that is limited to students' knowledge of isolated facts and skills and toward the assessment of students' growth in mathematical power.

The validation of students' achievement is not simple. To evaluate students' achievement, teachers or other evaluators summarize evidence from multiple sources to make judgments about students' development of mathematical power. The inferences are made by considering all the information about students' mathematical learning and by assigning value to the students' accomplishments. A primary consideration is to determine whether these inferences are appropriate.

The purpose of evaluating a student's achievement in mathematics is to open a public window on that student's mathematical thinking processes. This is a fair process when appropriate evidence of the student's learning is selected and appropriate inferences are made regarding the student's understanding. It is crucial that formal reports of students' accomplishments be based on evidence that accurately reflects the progress of each student toward the attainment of mathematical power. Not only do inferences need to be based on mathematical content that is important, but they also must be derived from learning situations in which students are actively engaged.

Example: Gaining Insight from Open-Ended Questions

Equity Standard: How does the assessment provide alternative activities or modes of response that invite each student to engage in the mathematics being assessed? How does the design of the assessment enable all students to exhibit what they know and can do?

Sources of evidence need not be limited to what may be easily assessed. However, in seeking to create a balanced variety of tasks to judge what students know and can do, it is important to acknowledge that the format of tasks can have important, often conflicting, effects on students. For example, open-ended questions are typically more language-dependent than multiple-choice questions, both in the statement of the problem and in the expected student responses. Although students who have a limited command of English might prefer multiple-choice items because these do not require explanations, incomplete evidence from short-answer or multiple-choice items may lead to inappropriate inferences. Conversely, the language demands of open-ended questions contrast with their potential for allowing students to select from a variety of mathematical representations (pictures, graphs, tables, charts, diagrams, models, symbols, formulas) to demonstrate their understanding. Such a multiplicity of representations can be less language-dependent, provide broader access, allow for greater diversity in solution strategies, and support more complete demonstrations of students' understanding than multiple-choice items.

Open-ended questions frequently offer more insight into students' thoughts than multiple-choice questions do. For example, what inferences can be made from each of the two students' responses about odd and even numbers shown in figure 14?

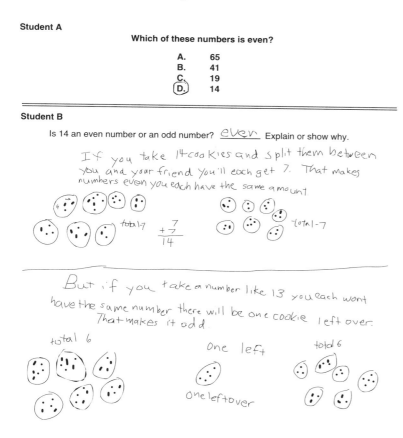

Student A

Which of these numbers is even?

    A.   65
    B.   41
    C.   19
    (D.)   14

Student B

Is 14 an even number or an odd number? _even_ Explain or show why.

If you take 14 cookies and split them between you and your friend you'll each get 7. That makes numbers even you each have the same amount.

total-7   +7 / 14   total -7

But if you take a number like 13 you each wont have the same number there will be one cookie left over. That makes it odd.

total 6   One left   total 6

One leftover

Fig. 14. Multiple-choice and open-ended questions about even numbers (response from Student B contributed by Patsy Higdon, Buncombe County, N.C., Public Schools)

Clearly, the response from student B provides more evidence of the student's understanding of even and odd numbers than it is possible to infer from the answer given by student A. The student's pictorial representations enhance the response and demonstrate the student's mathematical power.

CERTIFICATION FROM BALANCED SOURCES OF DATA

When students reach expected levels of performance, their achievements are often publicly and officially recognized in a variety of ways by their school, district, or community. Most typically, students graduate and are awarded diplomas or certificates of graduation. Sometimes, students get certificates, which verify that they have reached certain specified program goals. For example, at the end of high school, students may be certified to have reached specified levels of achievement by passing certain examinations. If students participate in mathematics competitions, their performances are recognized by special awards.

Where examinations are used to certify achievement, they are often designed by, and administered on behalf of, external persons or agencies. Although the format and structure of these examinations vary in a number of ways, there are three related problems with many of these tests. First, many examinations lack balance in the type of tasks they present. Second, many of them require students to give rapid responses in a limited time to numerous questions requiring the use of techniques that are presumed to have been well learned. For example, the Mathematics Level I and Level II sections of the SAT consist of fifty multiple-choice questions to be answered in an hour (1.2 minutes for each question). Similarly, in 1994 the American High School Mathematics Examination consisted of thirty questions to be answered in ninety minutes (3 minutes for each question). Such time-limited, multiple-choice examinations may assess some important skills but are limiting in that they fail to include opportunities for students to demonstrate their capability to use those skills to solve nonroutine problems. Third, because of their social importance, the message sent to teachers and students by this type of examination is that it is the rapid use of well-learned techniques that is most important These three problems are of particular concern with respect to minimal competency tests because they perpetuate a sterile image of mathematics to so many students. Such examinations fail to meet either the Mathematics Standards or the Learning Standards.

Some examinations given for certification in other countries and in international competitions provide examples of more complex problems. Chantal Shafroth's (1993) study of high school leaving examinations in several industrialized nations found that they are typically composed of a few independent problems, each made up of several parts, and that the time allocated to answer each part was more than ten minutes. For example, the mathematics examination for liberal arts students in the Netherlands consists of four problems each with four parts to be completed in three hours. Similarly, Japan's University Entrance Center Examination (UECE) has a two-part, sixty-minute mathematics examination in which Part 1 has six problems and Part 2 has five problems—each problem asks several questions of increasing complexity (Wu 1993). This allows students to demonstrate what they can do on every problem while probing their depth of understanding. Although examinations given in international competitions vary in a number of ways, most contain a small number of complex problems, with solutions judged by a jury that may rate responses on the clarity of presentation, reasoning used, and mathematical elegance in the solution process, in addition to accuracy of solution. For example, the International Mathematical Olympiad requires that each competitor complete a total of six problems during a two-day period.

Example: A Balanced Assessment System

The certification of a student's depth of understanding of mathematics through external examinations is an important purpose of assessment, but it needs to be based on a more balanced set of important questions than, until recently, was common in the United States. It is encouraging to know that several states (e.g., California, Connecticut, Kentucky, Maryland, Vermont, Wisconsin) are in the process of changing their state testing programs to be more balanced than in the past by including performance tasks, projects, or portfolios in their programs. Similarly, other states (e.g., Illinois, Minnesota) are expecting local school districts to develop such systems. Also, for Title I programs all states will be expected to develop more balanced assessment systems in the next few years.

An example of a certification process that achieves this balance and is in place is the Victorian Certificate of Education (VCE) from Victoria, Australia.

Victorian Certificate of Education

Secondary school students in Victoria who wish to be certified by the state as mathematics specialists must complete a complex assessment during their twelfth year of school. The VCE mathematics assessment is designed to complement the curriculum and assessment frameworks of the VCE instructional program.

The aims and content of the VCE program are defined by three related components: mathematical areas, essential mathematical activities, and learning activities (work requirements). The mathematical areas include algebra, arithmetic, calculus, coordinate geometry, geometry, logic, probability, statistics, and trigonometry. Essential mathematical activities include abstracting, inventing, proving, applying, and problem solving. Mathematical learning activities (work requirements) include conducting investigative projects; solving unfamiliar and nonstandard problems; using mathematical modeling as a tool in applying mathematical knowledge to real-world problems; and learning, practicing, and applying skills in standard situations. These curricular components are integrated into three instructional blocks offered to students in their final year of high school: Further Mathematics, Mathematical Methods, and Specialist Mathematics (Victorian Board of Studies 1994). The VCE assessment framework specifies that the package of assessment tasks in the VCE is to (1) be appropriate to the aims and content of the program; (2) reflect achievement in a variety of competencies, fields of knowledge, and activities; (3) provide reliable information and allow comparisons of students' performances; and (4) involve a judicious mix of school, moderated, and external assessments (Stephens and McCrae in press).

In both Further Mathematics and Mathematical Methods, students are required to complete an investigative project over a four-week period. This Common Assessment Task requires students to select one of three centrally set topics on which to base a report. In Specialist Mathematics, the VCE Common Assessment Task consists of two parts: a problem-solving task and a timed test. The student is allowed to choose one problem-solving task from among three offered and is then given approximately ten days to complete a report. An example of one of the problem-solving tasks (with Australian spelling) is given in figure 15.

Within a week after turning in the problem-solving task, the student must take a test that consists of several questions that are related to the problem-solving task chosen. For a student who had chosen the art gallery task, the timed (75 minutes) test questions in figure 16 would be required.

The scoring of the two parts of the common assessment task is done by a group of teachers using analytic schemes. For the problem-solving task, the student's report is analyzed on ten criteria (see

Mathematics Standard: Assess important content.

Problem 1

The Art Gallery

Question 1

A room in an art gallery contains a picture which you are interested in viewing. The picture is two metres high and is hanging so that the bottom of the picture is one metre above your eye level.

How far from the wall on which the picture is hanging should you stand so that the angle of vision occupied by the picture is a maximum? What is this maximum angle?

Question 2

On the opposite wall there is another equally interesting picture which is only one metre high and which is also hanging with its base one metre above eye level, directly opposite the first picture. Where should you stand to maximise your angle of vision of this second picture?

Question 3

How much advantage would a person 20 centimetres taller than you have in viewing these two pictures?

Question 4

This particular art-gallery room is six metres wide. A gallery guide of the same height as you wishes to place a viewing stand one metre high in a fixed position which provides the best opportunity for viewing both pictures simply by turning around. The guide decides that this could best be done by finding the position where the sum of the two angles of vision is greatest. Show that the maximum value which can be obtained by this approach does not give a suitable position for the viewing stand.

Question 5

The gallery guide then decides to adopt an alternative approach which makes the difference between the angles of vision of the two pictures, when viewed from the viewing stand, as small as possible. Where should the viewing stand be placed using this approach? Comment on your answer.

Fig. 15. A problem-solving task (Victorian Board of Studies 1994)

Test 1

Ice Hockey

This test is to be attempted by students who completed the art gallery problem-solving task (Problem 1).

Ice hockey is a team game played on an ice rink, in which players try to get the puck (a rubber disk) into the opposition goal. The goals are actually six feet in width (1.83 metres), but to simplify the arithmetic in this problem, they shall be assumed to be two metres wide.

Question 1

A player is moving in a straight line perpendicular to the line of the goal and 6 metres away from a parallel line through the centre of the goal (see diagram below). When the player is 10 metres from the goal line, what is the angle which the goal provides for aiming as seen from the player's point of view? (This is angle y in the diagram.)

Question 2

If the distance of the player from the goal line is x metres (rather than 10) find an expression for the tangent of the angle which the goal provides. By differentiating this expression with respect to x, or otherwise, show that this angle never exceeds 10 degrees. Explain why it is sufficient to differentiate tan y with respect to x rather than having to find dy/dx.

Question 3

Within what range of values of x must the player shoot in order that the angle provided by the goal (angle y) is greater than, or equal to, 8°.

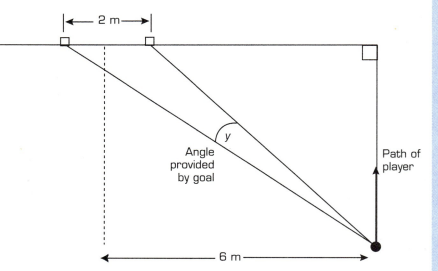

Fig. 16. A timed test (Victorian Board of Studies 1994)

fig. 17) and judged to be high, medium, or low. Teachers are also given the opportunity to make comments on the scoring sheet to explain the grades they choose. For 1995, this grading scale has been expanded to a five-point scale: Very High, High, Medium, Low, Very Low. "Not Shown" is also available.

	High	Med	Low	Not Shown
1. Identifying important information, and making and explaining any assumptions	☐	☐	☐	☐
2. Degree of mathematical formulation of problem	☐	☐	☐	☐
3. Analyzing information	☐	☐	☐	☐
4. Interpreting and evaluating results	☐	☐	☐	☐
5. Appropriate use of mathematical language, symbols and conventions	☐	☐	☐	☐
6. Correct and accurate use of mathematics	☐	☐	☐	☐
7. Appropriateness of mathematics used	☐	☐	☐	☐
8. Formulating valid conclusions	☐	☐	☐	☐
9. Quality of the account of the problem-solving activity	☐	☐	☐	☐
10. Depth of analysis shown	☐	☐	☐	☐

Fig. 17. Criteria for the award of grades (Victorian Board of Studies 1994)

Both the problem-solving task and the timed test are scored and then a weighted score becomes the student's grade. The task accounts for 60 percent of the final grade and the test for 40 percent. If there is a wide discrepancy between the two scores, the state board requires an interview with the student. The purpose of the interview is to give the student an opportunity to show that he or she understands the mathematics and can explain what is written in his or her report so that it can be authenticated by the school. All students are given trial versions of the tasks in advance so they will be familiar with the format and types of questions that might be asked.

The Victoria Certificate is an example of an external validation system that relies on more than one source of evidence. It gives students the opportunity to demonstrate their ability to solve an extended problem as well as to work under timed conditions. It also makes use of teachers' judgments in the scoring and grading.

PUBLIC PROFILES OF ACHIEVEMENT

When assessment is based on multiple sources of evidence and those sources yield rich information about what mathematics students know, what mathematics they can do, and their disposition toward mathematics, a single letter or number grade cannot adequately represent the breadth and depth of this information. Detailed profiles of a student's progress toward the goals that have been mutually set would be a better way of reporting information about the student's achievement. Of course, there are some instances for which a simplified summary is essential, but when students' performance data are collapsed into one score or

Inferences Standard: Assessments that are based on important mathematics, use multiple sources of evidence, minimize bias, and support students' learning provide the evidence needed for valid inferences about the mathematics students know and can do.

grade, it should only be used with caution and with an awareness that much information is lost during the process. Furthermore, the method of deriving such a grade should always be public.

Openness Standard: How do students become familiar with the assessment process and with the purposes, performance criteria, and consequences of the assessment?

Openness suggests that all parties involved have a clear understanding of the expectations of students' achievement and the criteria for evaluating students' progress toward these expectations. There are no secrets or hidden agendas. Specifically, all parties responsible for evaluation should be able to answer these questions:

♦ What mathematics will be assessed?

♦ What are the criteria for making judgments?

♦ How will the students' achievement be evaluated?

♦ How will the results be used?

Example: Descriptive Summary Reports

Traditional grading practices have endured primarily because they are convenient. They have offered teachers and schools a seemingly simple way to communicate to students and the public some information about what students know in an easily recognizable form. In fact, present practice does not serve students well because it ignores rich and varied information about what students know and can do in mathematics. Coming up with alternative models for grading will require that schools reexamine some of their basic assumptions about assessment and then make decisions about how the information gathered about students to monitor their progress should be synthesized, evaluated, and reported. Models need to be developed that describe students' progress toward performance criteria and that retain, to the greatest extent possible, the breadth and depth of evidence gathered from multiple sources. The summary report of the "Work Sampling System" (Meisels et al. 1993) is an example of such a system.

Summary evaluations of student achievement that are more descriptive than traditional grades need to be developed.

Work sampling system

Work sampling is a performance assessment system designed to document children's knowledge, behavior, and accomplishment as displayed in the classroom. It consists of three components: (1) developmental checklists, which are designed to systematize teachers' observations and documentation of the growth and progress of individual children; (2) portfolios, which are purposeful collections of children's work designed to illustrate and document each child's experience throughout the year; and (3) summary reports (fig. 18), which provide a means of synthesizing the rich information from the checklists and portfolios and communicating it in a meaningful way to parents, teachers, and administrators.

In the summary reports, the teacher synthesizes and evaluates a child's achievement in a variety of ways. In the Checklist rating, the teacher judges whether a child is developing as expected or needs development with respect to the established performance criteria described in the Checklist. The Portfolio rating reflects the child's development compared to classroom expectations based on evidence accumulated in the portfolio. In the Progress rating, the teacher judges whether the child is progressing as expected. In addition, space is allowed for brief comments

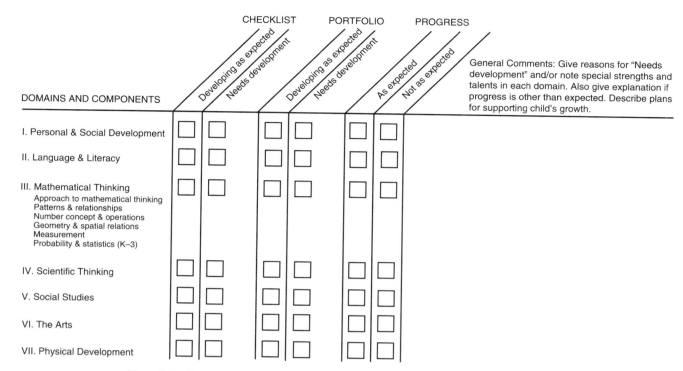

Fig. 18. Summary report (adapted from Meisels et al. 1993)

about the child's work and progress. Together, these multiple ratings and comments provide parents with rich, yet easily understood, information about their child's progress.

Ideally, data collected for summary evaluations will reveal no systematic differences related to characteristics such as family income level, gender, able-bodiedness, ethnicity, or geographic location. Teacher-, self-, or peer-monitoring of assessment practices is useful in helping to ensure equity for all students. Summary evaluations enable teachers to reflect on their practices in the classroom. By studying the information in summary reports, teachers can identify differences in performances by students or groups of students. These data furnish insights into needed instructional changes by helping to answer questions such as these:

♦ Does our school have the same high expectations for all students?

♦ Is our school providing all its students the opportunities they need to perform to the standards we have set?

SUMMARY

Using the Assessment Standards in evaluating students' achievement can ensure that inferences are trustworthy and that the process is equitable and open. Comparing students' performance with openly set criteria, concentrating on evidence of students' mathematical power, relying on balanced and multiple sources of evidence, and reporting results as profiles of achievement are practices that can improve summary reports of students' achievement.

PURPOSE: EVALUATING PROGRAMS

A program evaluation judges the quality and success of the program.

The primary question to be answered in any program evaluation is, How well is the program working in relation to goals and expectations for the students? With a school mathematics program, the question is, How well does it achieve the vision of the Curriculum, Evaluation, Teaching, and Assessment Standards? The term *program* is used here to refer to any significant unit of instruction. Examples of programs include a thematic unit involving ratio and proportion, a course involving precalculus mathematics, all the mathematics courses at a middle school, a district's mathematics curriculum, and the implementation of a state mathematics framework across schools and districts.

The Assessment Standards represent criteria with which to judge the quality of mathematics assessments, whether in a full program evaluation or as assessment components within a program. Evaluating the assessment components of a program involves making judgments about how well they provide information for such educational purposes as monitoring students' progress, supporting teachers' instructional decisions, and evaluating students' achievement—topics discussed elsewhere in this document. The discussion in this section deals with the use of assessments as a source of information for evaluating programs.

A program evaluation uses student performance data with other evidence to judge the quality and success of the program. Information on students' achievement produced through assessment may be used for making decisions about continuing a program or for making modifications in an ongoing program. Many questions about such programs can be answered by directly assessing students' knowledge of mathematics as they progress through the program.

The Evaluation Standards called for increased attention to "[e]valuating the program by systematically collecting information on outcomes, curriculum, and instruction."
—NCTM (1989, p. 191)

However, a program evaluation is more than a set of student assessment results. In addition to the evaluation of students' learning, program evaluations include information about other important elements, such as goals, curriculum materials, instructional methods, a student's opportunity to learn, and responsibilities of teachers and administrators. The *Curriculum and Evaluation Standards for School Mathematics* included four Evaluation Standards related to program evaluation (i.e., Indicators for Program Evaluation, Curriculum and Instructional Resources, Instruction, and Evaluation Team) that furnished criteria for constructing a mathematics program evaluation system. This discussion on evaluation complements those concepts while focusing on the use of the Assessment Standards in program evaluation. Another resource, *A Guide for Reviewing School Mathematics Programs* (Blume and Nicely 1991), offers step-by-step suggestions for conducting a mathematics program evaluation and poses detailed questions about the important elements in such an evaluation.

Assessment provides evidence for judging the quality of educational programs of various sizes.

A close connection exists between assessment for the purpose of making educational decisions and assessment for the purpose of evaluating programs. Among the objectives for each is the accumulation of evidence that can be used to judge the quality of educational programs. However, programs differ significantly in scale, and a program evaluation has many other objectives as well. An individual teacher often uses assessments to make decisions about portions of the curriculum on a relatively short-term basis—decisions that serve as immediate guides for instruction in his or her classroom. Similarly, teachers at an individual school may evaluate the effectiveness of the mathematics program at their school by assessing students' achievement and gathering evidence of opportunities offered by the program for students to achieve the goals emphasized in the school. In contrast, a program evaluation team uses assessments to make decisions about a larger portion of the curriculum or about instructional practices over an extended period of time, and the resulting decisions may influence the work of students and teachers in many classrooms or schools.

Teachers have the opportunity to assume new roles as leaders in expanding the linkages among curriculum, instruction, and assessment in their mathematics programs. Teachers need to be valued participants in evaluation teams in all phases, from planning assessment activities and gathering evidence to interpreting evidence and using results. Although an evaluation team at the district, state or province, or national level may include administrators, mathematics specialists, school board members, parents, and business and community leaders, it must also include teachers.

Teachers have the opportunity to assume new roles as leaders in expanding the linkages among curriculum, instruction, and assessment in a program evaluation.

Consistent with the NCTM's vision of reform, the Assessment Standards suggest that several shifts in program evaluation practice may be necessary:

♦ Toward making program decisions based on high-quality evidence from multiple sources and away from relying on over-simplified evidence from a single test or test format

♦ Toward detailed analyses of group data (e.g., examining variations in responses, and the disaggregation of data) and away from reporting only group means

♦ Toward using the professional judgments of teachers about students' performances along with other evidence and away from relying primarily on externally derived evidence

USING A VARIETY OF HIGH-QUALITY EVIDENCE

For program evaluation, it is incumbent on the evaluator—whether an individual or an evaluation team—to look at the sources and quality of evidence that indicate students' progress toward the program's goals. Two primary sources of information are—

♦ data from assessment instruments created for the purpose of evaluating the program;

♦ data from classroom assessment practices already in place.

To be useful for program evaluation, it must be clear that both sources of evidence are aligned with the program's goals and standards for the mathematics in the program. Evaluators must also furnish the quality of evidence needed to make valid inferences about students' opportunities to learn and their accomplishment of the program's goals.

Coherence Standard: Assessments must be aligned with the program's goals.

One distinction between the use of assessment information for program evaluation and its use for other educational purposes is that program decisions can be made using results from groups of students; complete performances by all students in a classroom or school are not needed for this purpose. There are several implications of this condition for program evaluation. Matrix sampling—under which any student sees only a sample of the tasks, or any task is answered by only a sample of students—can be used to estimate group performance. This has two potential benefits: First, it can minimize the cost and amount of instructional time required for an external assessment; and, second, and most important, it makes it possible to expand the scope and types of tasks that can be administered to students.

For example, some years ago the California Assessment Program (CAP) assessed all sixth-grade students in the state by giving each a subset of the 360 mathematics questions about which CAP wished to collect information. Because each student responded to only 12 items, the test required a minimum of classroom time to administer, but the data yielded estimates of group performance on a wide variety of mathematical topics. The National Assessment of Educational Progress (NAEP) has long used this technique to derive estimates of student performance for the nation (and recently for participating states). Similarly, the New Standards Project is currently deriving estimates of group performance on a number of extended performance tasks through sampling. Individual students' scores on such tests are not useful for program evaluation; however, estimates of group scores at the school, district, state or provincial, or even national level are meaningful. Note that although this assessment technique is potentially a very powerful tool for program evaluation, it is just a tool. The quality of the evaluation can be judged by using the Assessment Standards to examine the tasks included, the methods of profiling and reporting results, and other assessment-related features of the evaluation process.

A variety of complex tasks and more economical tests can be appropriately used together.

In conjunction with such sampling techniques, a variety of complex tasks and more economical tests can be appropriately used together without taking away too much instructional time from any one student, class, or teacher. Short-answer or multiple-choice tests (or other machine-scorable tests) can elicit some information on skills if the balance among topics is appropriate for the intended purpose. In addition, performance assessment tasks can indicate how well students are able to integrate their knowledge of mathematics and apply this knowledge in different situations if the contexts are familiar to the students. Group problem solving can also reveal students' communication strengths and experience in working with others if the students have routinely participated in group problem solving.

Readily available tests may be poorly suited to the particular program to be evaluated.

A frequent problem with selecting a collection of assessment tasks appropriate for evaluating a program is that readily available tests may be poorly suited to the particular program being evaluated. Throughout the design, administration, and reporting phases of the assessment process, evaluators make important decisions that are specific to the circumstances. Because evaluators make those decisions with particular purposes in mind, it is problematic if they select an assessment designed for one purpose and apply it to another. For example, an assessment developed by one state to evaluate the implementation of its mathematics framework, which emphasizes trigonometry from a circular-function perspective, is not well suited for the evaluation of a program designed to closely match another state's framework that has been designed to emphasize trigonometry from a triangle perspective. The Assessment Standards point out other considerations that must be satisfied in selecting appropriate assessments for particular purposes.

Example: Program Selection

A number of different mathematics programs are available to teachers in any school at any given time. How can school staffs decide which program is best suited to their students' needs? From among the high-quality programs that reflect the Curriculum Standards and the Teaching Standards, one seeks those that best match both the students and the community being served, as well as the teachers who will teach the program. Some of the issues that arise in selecting programs are illustrated in the following example.

Mathematics Standard: How does the assessment elicit the use of mathematics that is important to know and be able to do? What inferences about students' mathematical knowledge, understanding, thinking processes, and dispositions can be made from the assessment?

Tough Choices

The kindergarten and first-grade teachers at Rolling Meadows Elementary School were preparing to pilot-test two mathematics programs. The teachers were discussing how they would go about evaluating the two programs to make a decision about which program to adopt for use the following year. They all agreed that the most important thing to consider was the mathematics content and the processes that the children were learning in each program.

"This would be easy if these were older children," noted Katie West. "We could just give all the kids a test at the end of the year and see which kids did better. Then we would know which program was better."

"But," cautioned Markel Whitten, "what would you put on the test? If one program emphasizes a particular topic, such as patterning, or a particular process, such as reasoning, the children who were taught in that program would do better on that part of the test."

Mathematics Standard: What mathematics is reflected in the assessment?

"Perhaps we should give the children a series of activities to do that match our mathematics curriculum standards and see which children do better on those activities," said Maria Gonzales.

Coherence Standard: How does the assessment match the curriculum and instructional practice?

"I still think we would need to look at more than just scores on a set of activities," said Markel again. "I think that throughout the year we should each collect examples of students' work that are representative of what the children are learning in the program. It would be sort of like making a portfolio for the program. By making a program portfolio, we could show the other teachers what mathematics content and mathematical processes are part of each program. Examples of a variety of student work—projects, writings, drawings, and on-demand activities—would show what the children learned during the school year."

Inferences Standard: What evidence about learning does the assessment provide? What multiple sources of evidence are used for making inferences, and how is the evidence used?

"Each of us could also keep some anecdotal records about the children's attitudes and dispositions toward mathematics," added Jayne Jackson.

Used with permission from the Wisconsin Center for Education Research, School of Education, University of Wisconsin—Madison

The teachers then decided that they would work together to create a program portfolio for each program. The portfolios would contain examples of students' work throughout the year, results from activities that measured progress toward content standards, and teachers' anecdotal records. The teachers would then use the portfolios and program materials to compare each program to the district's curriculum standards to make a decision about which program to adopt.

This example involved a yearlong program evaluation. Evaluations over shorter periods must particularly consider the increased effects of such factors as the initial struggles with a new program or the time it takes to become familiar with the program's features. Although the example focused on a program evaluation by teachers at a single school, relevant evidence from additional sites can also be helpful in program evaluations.

Different mathematics programs have different goals as well as different outcomes. Program selection, therefore, involves at least three steps: (1) setting program goals, (2) determining—partially through the assessment of students' learning—the extent to which each program helps students achieve its goals, and (3) choosing the program that yields the greatest progress toward the goals most valued. The Assessment Standards should be used in the program-selection process to judge the adequacy of the assessment of students' learning. In the preceding example, the teachers would need to examine the use of portfolios (how items are selected for inclusion and how they are judged) in light of the Assessment Standards.

As choices are made among mathematics programs, one needs to remember that a program cannot be evaluated apart from the situation in which it will be used. On the one hand, a program that looks good on paper or in a tryout may not work well when it is implemented on a large scale. On the other hand, interested teachers can take a program that does not seem to be working well elsewhere and make it effective in their classrooms. The process of program selection needs to be seen both as a selection issue and as an issue involving modification for a specific context. The Assessment Standards should be used to verify the quality of the evidence about students' performance when making such decisions.

DETAILED ANALYSES OF GROUP DATA

Too often, the success or failure of a mathematics program is based on overall mean scores from a norm-referenced test or on a district-by-district comparison produced from a statewide assessment. Program evaluators are encouraged to use the Assessment Standards to examine the items in such tests and the ways in which data are analyzed and reported. It is important to scrutinize such tests carefully, even when the data are to be aggregated for program evaluation purposes. The test characteristics should be consistent with the information needed for the evaluation of the particular program. Individual problems should elicit the kinds of student performances that are in alignment with the important goals of the program. Collections of items should balance the evidence of students' understanding with the relative emphases given to the various goals of the program. The relevant information an assessment can provide is often limited by the choice of question formats. For example, multiple-choice questions are poorly suited to furnishing information on problem solving and mathematical communication. Tests that use primarily multiple-choice questions often limit the scope of what is being tested to what fits the multiple-choice format.

Many tests in current use provide insufficient information for making program decisions.

In addition, many large-scale tests report too little information. For example, simply to report school means (often average percentiles) can be deceiving. Means do not convey information about the dispersion of scores being averaged. Knowing that a class averaged 65 percent correct answers on a district test provides very little evidence for making decisions—some undoubtedly score higher and some much lower. How many students scored higher, and how much lower did other students score? Moreover, the average of 65 percent does not tell us that the students are doing satisfactorily on *all* the curriculum components that are assessed. In some components they may be strong and in some weak; one simply cannot make these distinctions on the basis of an average.

Often a meaningful disaggregation of the data is warranted. Prudent disaggregation and reorganization of the data can help answer a great many questions about how the program is serving—or failing to serve—its students. To continue the 65 percent example, one might have questions about the student population, such as, Are boys and girls succeeding equally well in the program? Are students of all ethnicities showing the same progress? To answer questions like these, the assessment results can be disaggregated to derive scores for each subgroup of interest. Another way to disaggregate data is by mathematical content. Assessment data are often reported globally under the heading "mathematics." Examining the data in light of important content areas can point to particular strengths and weaknesses in students' learning and, in turn, shed light on the strengths and weaknesses of the program.

In program evaluation, a disaggregation of assessment data is often warranted.

Because evidence about students' performance is often used to judge programs, assessors need to scrutinize the assessment materials they use. Furthermore, they need to conduct detailed analyses of the derived group data. The use of student performance data should be judged against each of the six Assessment Standards to ensure that only high-quality evidence is considered in the program evaluation process.

Example: Analyzing Scores

This example illustrates how the report of scores from a statewide assessment can convey two very different messages, depending on how they are analyzed.

Reporting assessment results aggregated over a group of students or a set of activities can misrepresent the adequacy of the program in serving the mathematical needs of subgroups of students.

Going beyond the Mean

A state administered a mathematics knowledge and concept test to all its grade 11 students. Results for each school district were reported in the local newspaper. The graph in figure 19 represents the results for one district and shows the district mean and the range of school means within the district for the last four years.

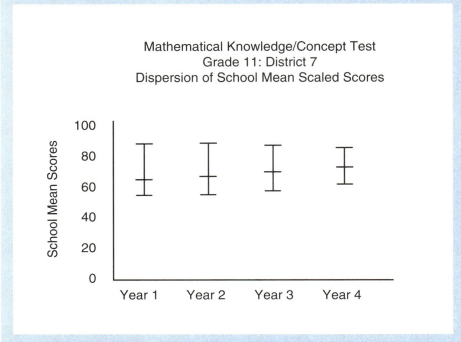

Fig. 19. District mean and range of school means

Inference Standard: What multiple sources of evidence are used for making inferences, and how is the evidence used? What is the value of the evidence for each use?

Coherence Standard: How does the assessment match its purposes and its uses?

Openness Standard: What access do those affected by the assessment have to tasks, scoring goals, performance criteria, and samples of students' work that have been scored and discussed?

When the graph appeared in the newspaper, it was accompanied by a statement from the district superintendent, who emphasized improved achievement over the four years: "Each year our average score has increased."

The superintendent was not pleased with the results, however, and put a discussion of the test results on the agenda for the next district staff meeting. She intended to explore the shrinking range evident in the data and the possible causes for the narrowing of the distribution of school scores while the district mean was increasing.

The district mathematics supervisor was interested in a further analysis of the scores by school, so she planned a discussion of the test results for the next mathematics department faculty meeting at each school. Prior to the series of meetings, she obtained the student scores for each school in the district for the previous four years. The frequency distribution of scores for the most recent year from one of the schools is shown in figure 20.

At the mathematics department meeting for East High School, members of the group drew some specific conclusions about students' learning by analyzing the district-level data with the frequency distributions for their school. They began by asking a question from the Inferences Standard: What evidence about learning does the assessment provide? Although they knew that the mean and median scores for the district had steadily increased over the previous four years, the frequency distributions during that time indicated that the percentage of students in their school scoring above 85 percent had actually decreased. Also, in the most recent year, 25 percent of their students scored 50 percent or less, well below the rest of the students in the school.

Equity Standard: To what sources can differences in performance be attributed?

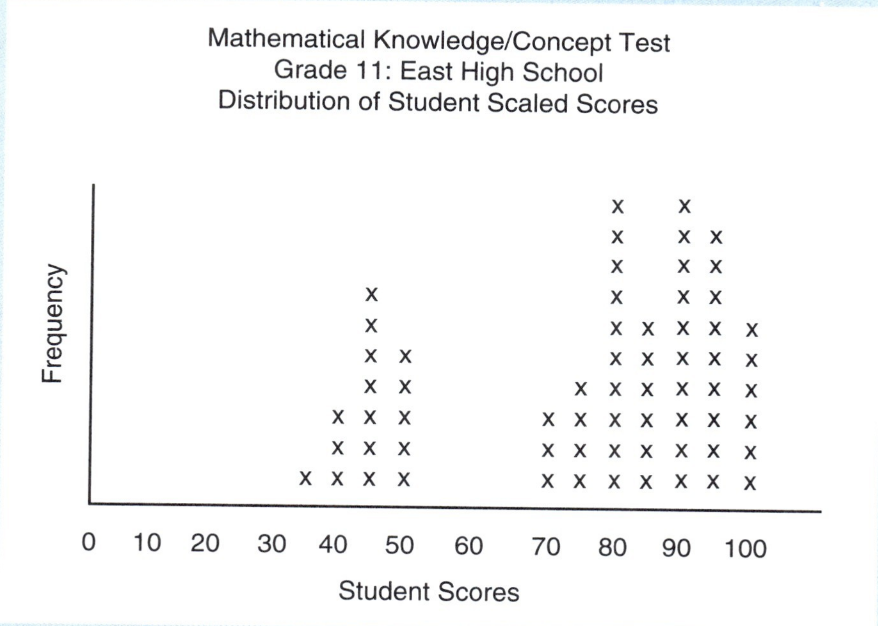

Mathematical Knowledge/Concept Test
Grade 11: East High School
Distribution of Student Scaled Scores

Fig. 20. Distribution of student scores for one school

The faculty members recognized that looking solely at summary information for the district could lead them astray in making decisions based on schoolwide performance. Supported by a detailed analysis of all the information available, they decided that two actions were required. First, the group made specific plans to attend more appropriately to the needs of students who scored in the lower quartile. Second, the group decided to gather additional information and do some further analysis of why the number of students scoring above 85 percent had decreased. If the state assessment was unable to furnish enough information to answer this question, they would gather the appropriate evidence themselves.

By presenting the frequency distributions for that school, the district mathematics supervisor showed that an analysis of all the available data resulted in a very different picture of students' mathematics achievement than the district-level summary printed in the newspaper. Without such an analysis, one could be led to the invalid inference that the students in the district were showing steady and continuous improvement in mathematics. The frequency distributions, however, enabled the mathematics faculty to conclude that its mathematics program was not serving all its students well and pointed to the need for additional information.

Example: Understanding Variations in Performance

The following example illustrates the importance of examining other subsets of assessment data, such as scores by mathematical topics, to assure that program evaluation decisions are appropriate.

Performance Puzzles

The mathematics assessment committee in a school district was conducting an evaluation of its K–6 mathematics program. This committee was composed of the district mathematics specialist and two teachers from each school. One piece of data under consideration was a performance test the committee had designed and administered expressly for the program evaluation. The test results indicated that 62 percent of the fourth graders had demonstrated adequate performance on all the district's mathematics goals for the areas of measurement and data analysis.

The committee decided to disaggregate the data in several ways to learn more about what this 62 percent might mean. Two ways the data were disaggregated were by major content topic and by school. Part of the disaggregated data is shown in the chart in figure 21.

	Measurement	Data Analysis
Canyon Creek	44%	60%
Jefferson	72%	33%
Greenbriar	42%	64%

Fig. 21. Scores by mathematical topic

To try to understand the variations in performance scores better, the committee met with teachers and administrators at each school to discuss the data. The disaggregation of data provided the detailed information the committee members needed in order to focus their discussions on some of the questions suggested by the Equity Standard.

What opportunities did each student at Canyon Creek Elementary School have to learn the mathematics that was being assessed? Reflecting on their curriculum, the teachers at Canyon Creek Elementary School noted that their students had not had many experiences with measurement during the school year. The committee made specific plans to help all the teachers at Canyon Creek explore approaches that would ensure that all their students had the experi-

Inferences Standard: Can inferences be improved by a closer inspection of the assessment data?

Equity Standard: The disaggregation of data can lead to more informed judgments about students' opportunities to learn what was assessed.

ence needed to apply basic measurement processes to everyday problems.

How did the design of the assessment enable all students at Jefferson Elementary School to exhibit what they knew and could do? A significant number of limited-English-proficiency students at Jefferson Elementary School were disadvantaged by the fact that the data analysis items required the students to write their analyses and support their conclusions in paragraph form. The committee made specific plans to modify the assessment to allow alternative ways for students to successfully communicate their understanding.

How did the conditions under which the assessment was administered enable all students at Greenbriar Elementary School to exhibit their mathematical power? Although the students at Greenbriar Elementary School had studied measurement as part of their curriculum, the test called for the students to weigh different objects on a pan balance. The school did not own any pan balances, so the children were forced to skip that question on the test. The committee made specific plans to acquire a set of pan balances for Greenbriar.

Mathematics Standard: How does the assessment engage students in realistic and worthwhile mathematical activities?

By meeting with school personnel and by disaggregating the assessment data by school and by content area, the program evaluators for the district were able to uncover some of the reasons that students in these schools did not perform as expected in particular content areas. Without looking at the data in this way, the committee might have concluded that all students in the district were meeting the standards for high achievement and that the performance test used to measure this achievement was adequate. However, the committee found that not all students were being given an opportunity to learn the important mathematics presented; thus, not all students were being given the opportunity to demonstrate their mathematical power.

Equity Standard: How does the design of the assessment enable all students to exhibit what they know and can do?

PROFESSIONAL JUDGMENTS OF TEACHERS

External written examinations were first instituted in the United States in the Boston schools in 1845 as a substitute for oral tests when enrollments became so large that school committees could no longer examine all pupils orally. Horace Mann, then secretary of the Massachusetts Board of Education, concluded that a written examination was superior to oral testing, in part because "it prevents the 'officious interference' of the teacher" and "it removes all possibility of favoritism" (Gerberich, Green, and Jorgensen 1962, p. 22). Since that time, many of the tests given in schools have been externally developed, administered, scored, and analyzed—their use justified on the basis of being impartial and fair to all students.

Although this attitude about teachers' judgments still persists in many circles, it is now recognized that "impartial" external tests can be both biased and constraining—biased in the sense that such tests often are not aligned with the actual curriculum that students have been taught, and constraining in the sense that the test items are designed to have only one possible unambiguous answer and that the time one has in which to produce an answer is limited. Such tests fail to meet several of the Assessment Standards.

Inferences Standard: How sensitive is the assessor to the demands the assessment makes and to unexpected responses?

Today, this situation is changing. As performance tasks, projects, and portfolios are being more widely used as the basis for evaluation by states and provinces, school districts, and school committees, teachers have become central players in developing new assessments, creating scoring rubrics, moderating students' scores, and implementing other aspects of new assessments. Teachers can and do make consistent judgments about the quality of assessment tasks and students' performances on a variety of complex tasks and about ways of using those results for evaluating programs.

Teachers should be involved in judging the quality of assessment tasks and students' performance.

Example: Using Assessment to Meet Students' Needs

A program needs to be sensitive to the needs of the students it serves. Many groups of students participate in school programs. As teachers and other evaluators use information from assessments to help improve the program, they need to be responsive to the needs of each group. The example below illustrates how assessment can influence a mathematics program for a group of high-achieving students.

Putting Choices in the Program

The mathematics teachers at Banneker High School were on their annual summer retreat where they were reviewing the previous year's mathematics program and planning for the next year. As the teachers were analyzing data pertaining to student achievement, Mr. Fernandez pointed out that once again there was a significant group of students at each grade level who were scoring well on nearly every measure of student achievement.

Coherence Standard: How do students view the connection between assessment and instruction?

"But," Mr. Washington interjected, "if we have so many students who are doing so well on these tests, why aren't we seeing them in our advanced mathematics classes?"

Mathematics Standard: How does the assessment engage students in realistic and worthwhile mathematical activities?

Mrs. Morton then relayed a story about her honors geometry students who said they were not interested in taking more mathematics courses because the classes were boring and irrelevant. Several other teachers nodded in agreement.

Inferences Standard: How is professional judgment used in making inferences about learning?

After additional anecdotes from their colleagues and more careful analysis of the mathematics content being taught and tested, the teachers decided they needed to restructure their course offerings. Instead of funneling mathematically talented students into courses that stressed acceleration, they felt that courses offering the students opportunities to broaden and deepen their understanding of significant mathematics content, such as discrete mathematics, topology, statistics, and probability, would be more appropriate.

Inferences Standard: What multiple sources of evidence are used for making inferences and how is the evidence used?

However, they decided that before they began restructuring courses, they would survey and possibly interview some of the students who were doing well in mathematics to see what types of courses would increase their interest in the continued study of mathematics.

The teachers recognized that reorganizing their course offerings would be a major task, would take a long time to complete, and would need continuing attention. However, the teachers all felt that

Used with permission from the Wisconsin Center for Education Research, School of Education, University of Wisconsin—Madison

by taking action, they could begin to make an impact immediately on a small scale in their own classes to enrich the opportunities they were offering their talented students.

As teachers and program evaluators work on improving the mathematics programs in a school or district, they often combine data from existing assessments with data from assessments tailored to a specific program. It is important that evaluators remain sensitive to the quality and appropriateness of their data sets with reference to each of the Assessment Standards.

SUMMARY

Program evaluation often involves high-stakes decisions for students, schools, districts, and states or provinces—decisions that affect classroom practice, curriculum, the organization of courses of study, teaching strategies, and the availability of instructional resources. The context and characteristics of a program evaluation need to be clearly communicated, the results carefully interpreted, and inferences validly crafted before important decisions are made.

Assessments play a vital role in program evaluation. Are those assessments meeting each of the six Assessment Standards? For example, when we consider the Mathematics and Learning Standards, we ask whether the assessments carried out in a program evaluation enhance the learning of the important mathematics in the school's curriculum. Very often, the perceived success or failure of a new mathematics program is based primarily on assessment information for students who have participated in the program. A mathematics program will be judged most appropriately when an evaluation applies the Assessment Standards to the evidence of students' achievement and of their opportunities to learn.

WHAT'S NEXT?

The *Assessment Standards* is for use by everyone who is or should be concerned with improving mathematics assessment. We challenge you to reflect on the six Assessment Standards and consider their implications for particular educational purposes. Used in conjunction with the NCTM's *Curriculum and Evaluation Standards* and *Professional Teaching Standards*, the *Assessment Standards* can be a powerful tool for examining and taking action on our educational problems. This can be done by engaging in dialogue to help construct an understanding of the standards, using the standards to identify your own assessment issues, reflecting on the role of the Assessment Standards in mathematics education reform, and acting to bring about change where it is needed.

The Standards *documents are tools, not solutions.*

Think of the assessment process as a problem-solving process. Developing a facility for solving mathematics problems requires experience in thinking, reasoning, planning, communicating, analyzing, and generalizing, plus developing the confidence and disposition to engage in problem solving. Similarly, the assessment process involves planning, gathering evidence, interpreting the evidence, and using the results.

For many, the reform of mathematics assessment has already begun. Teachers are using a variety of assessment methods to support their students' mathematical growth. Schools have taken up the challenge of redefining their learning goals to bring about greater alignment with the standards for curriculum, evaluation, and teaching. Districts and states and provinces have begun to develop alternative assessment systems. These efforts are laudable, and these reformers should be encouraged to continue. For them, the Assessment Standards can serve as criteria against which to judge their assessment efforts, and for all of us they can serve as guides for implementing high-quality assessment.

For many, the reform of mathematics assessment has already begun.

DIALOGUE

New ideas need to be discussed, thought about, and assimilated. Engaging in dialogue about the material presented here is an effective way to experience the power of the Assessment Standards. A dialogue might develop between you and a colleague, among members of a school committee, or between instructional leaders such as supervisors or principals. A dialogue might also occur between teacher and student or between teacher and parent. Or, a dialogue could begin among members of a district or a state or provincial committee. Whatever the form, engaging in dialogue with others about the assessment process can be a powerful way to achieve an understanding of the six standards and begin the change process. The questions at the end of each standard and the examples in this document can also be used to stimulate discussions.

Talking with colleagues can foster an understanding of the Assessment Standards and help develop a shared vision of what to assess and how to do it.

PERSONALIZATION

You and your colleagues will have your own set of assessment issues. Assimilating the ideas in this document includes applying them to your particular context. Many of us have multiple responsibilities, and thus we have multiple assessment issues to consider. Perhaps you are a classroom teacher who is concerned not only about your own classroom practice but also about school, district, or state or provincial assessment efforts. You might also be concerned about the ways in which student assessment results are used at your school and how those results are communicated to your students and their parents. Maybe you are a parent or caregiver who is concerned about how your children are assessed. If you are a school administrator, you have your own list of issues. Your understanding of the standards may be only academic, however, until it is made personal by applying them to the assessment concerns you have.

Personalize the Assessment Standards.

REFLECTION

As you reflect on the vision of alternative assessment practices suggested by this document, it is important to go beyond assessment and recognize the connections among assessment, curriculum, teaching, and learning. Use the standards to consider in an organized way the impact of assessment on all areas of school mathematics.

As you study this document, reflect on your personal experiences and practice, identify the goals you would like to reach, and become aware of the obstacles you may encounter. Don't become so concerned by the complexity of the suggested reforms that you are unable to begin the process. As you try new procedures, remember to start small, reflect on your progress, and then continue your efforts.

When trying new assessment procedures, start small, revise, and try again.

ACTION

How can you become involved in the process of educational reform? Educational reform is a recursive process. That is, the process begins with manageable steps, the results of which feed into the next round of reform. These Assessment Standards are intended to add impetus to the many changes occurring in educational practice—changes that have been discussed and illustrated throughout this document. The many shifts in practice suggested are summarized at the end of this section. To make optimal use of this document is to establish it among your personal guidelines for educational reform.

We contend that the assessment process, in all its phases, is a shared responsibility. There must be consensus in adopting the standards, and the process of using them requires mutual agreement. In particular, issues of accountability are much more explicit and powerful in standards-oriented assessment processes than in reform efforts that are not aligned with a standards-based structure. We share responsibility for using assessment to enhance the learning of mathematics for all students.

Assessment is a shared responsibility.

SUMMARIZING THE DOCUMENT: SHIFTS IN PRACTICE

The vision of these Assessment Standards can be realized in making shifts from current practice in school assessment toward the ideals portrayed in this document. Each shift represents movement along a continuum toward improved practice. Although these shifts summarize important ideas for changing assessment practices, they are not intended to be comprehensive, nor are they intended to stand alone. They highlight important ideas explained in this document.

FINAL COMMENT

Mathematics assessment reform, like mathematics curriculum reform and mathematics teaching reform, is a journey, not a destination. The *Standards* documents provide powerful shared statements for judging our progress on this journey in the company of others. Think of these documents as maps to guide the process. Our routes may differ, but the goal is the same: to develop mathematical power in *all* students.

Reform is a journey, not a destination.

MAJOR SHIFTS IN ASSESSMENT PRACTICE

TOWARD	AWAY FROM
◆ Assessing students' full mathematical power	◆ Assessing only students' knowledge of specific facts and isolated skills
◆ Comparing students' performance with established criteria	◆ Comparing students' performance with that of other students
◆ Giving support to teachers and credence to their informed judgment	◆ Designing "teacher-proof" assessment systems
◆ Making the assessment process public, participatory, and dynamic	◆ Making the assessment process secret, exclusive, and fixed
◆ Giving students multiple opportunities to demonstrate their full mathematical power	◆ Restricting students to a single way of demonstrating their mathematical knowledge
◆ Developing a shared vision of what to assess and how to do it.	◆ Developing assessment by oneself
◆ Using assessment results to ensure that all students have the opportunity to achieve their potential	◆ Using assessment to filter and select students out of the opportunities to learn mathematics
◆ Aligning assessment with curriculum and instruction	◆ Treating assessment as independent of curriculum or instruction
◆ Basing inferences on multiple sources of evidence	◆ Basing inferences on restricted or single sources of evidence
◆ Viewing students as active participants in the assessment process	◆ Viewing students as the objects of assessment
◆ Regarding assessment as continual and recursive	◆ Regarding assessment as sporadic and conclusive
◆ Holding all concerned with mathematics learning accountable for assessment results	◆ Holding only a few accountable for assessment results

ability The capacity to do something; the power to perform. In this document, ability emphasizes developed powers to perform, which are influenced through educational experiences as well as by natural talents, aptitudes, or traits.

access Rights and means to approach or engage in with understanding. Assessments provide for equal access when they include tasks that are shown to be equally appropriate for all students, allow multiple approaches and strategies, and accept multiple justifiable responses. See **open-ended questions.**

achievement Successful accomplishment or attainment of educational goals.

activities The cognitive functioning or physical actions in which students are engaged, whether by assignment or on their own initiative.

adequacy Ability to satisfy the requirements of the intended purposes and their consequences.

assessment The process of gathering evidence about a student's knowledge of, ability to use, and disposition toward mathematics and of making inferences from that evidence for a variety of purposes. *Assessment* is a term that has often been used interchangeably with the terms *testing, measurement,* and *evaluation,* or to distinguish between student assessment and program evaluation. In this document, assessment is used as defined above to emphasize understanding and description of both qualitative and quantitative evidence in making judgments and decisions. See **evaluation, measure, test.**

assessment standards Criteria for judging the quality of assessment practices, which embody a vision of assessment consistent with the Curriculum and the Teaching Standards derived from shared philosophies of mathematics, cognition, and learning.

authenticity The degree to which activities are faithful, comprehensive representations of the contexts and complexity found in important, real-life performances of adults that are nonroutine yet meaningful and engaging for students. Authentic activities are either replicas of or analogous to the kinds of problems faced by adult citizens or professionals in the field and are accompanied by the resources and opportunities for discussion, collaboration, revision, and justification typical of the production of quality adult performances (Wiggins 1993).

benchmarks Descriptions of student performances at various developmental levels that contribute to the achievement of performance standards.

bias Conditions in content, procedures, or interpretation of assessment information that favor one or more groups of participants over other groups.

coherence The quality of logical connection and orderly relationship of parts.

concepts General and fundamental ideas—for example, the ideas that are needed to guide reasoning, problem formulation, and problem solving in nonroutine situations.

consistency Compatibility or agreement among successive acts, ideas, or events.

context The circumstances or situation in which a mathematical problem occurs or in which mathematics can be applied.

credibility The quality of being plausible, believable, dependable, or worthy of confidence.

disposition Interest in, and appreciation for, mathematics; a tendency to think and act in positive ways; includes confidence, curiosity, perseverance, flexibility, inventiveness, and reflectivity in doing mathematics.

equal Having the same quantity, measure, value, privileges, status, or rights.

equality A state of uniformity in quantity, measure, value, privileges, status, or rights.

equitable assessment The degree to which the process of gathering evidence has provided opportunities equally appropriate for each student to demonstrate the valued thinking processes, knowledge, and skills that he or she has developed. Equitable assessment is not achieved by creating the same conditions for all students but rather by creating conditions that are appropriate to the same extent for each student.

equity The state or quality of being fair, just, equally appropriate for all students. See **equitable assessment.**

equivalent Equal in value or meaning, interchangeable, or having comparable effects.

evaluation The process of determining the worth of, or assigning a value to, something on the basis of careful examination and judgment. As used in this document, evaluation is one use of assessment information. See **assessment.**

framework An organizing system for, and arrangement of, the mathematical understanding, performances, and dispositions to be assessed, which will assist the planning of assessments.

generalizations Inferences or conclusions from many particulars of the evidence in hand, supported by a theory of the relationships between the particulars and the more general inferences or conclusions.

inferences Conclusions or assertions derived from evidence; deductions.

item A single, often decontextualized test question or problem.

judgments Authoritative estimates or opinions of quality, value, and other features, formed by distinguishing the relations among multiple sources of sound and reasonable evidence; formal decisions.

mathematical power "Mathematical power includes the ability to explore, conjecture, and reason logically; to solve nonroutine problems; to communicate about and through mathematics; and to connect ideas within mathematics and between mathematics and other intellectual activity. Mathematical power also involves the development of personal self-confidence and a disposition to seek, evaluate, and use quantitative and spatial information in solving problems and in making decisions. Students' flexibility, perseverance, interest, curiosity, and inventiveness also affect the realization of mathematical power" (NCTM 1991, p. 1).

measure To indicate how much of some specified, quantifiable unit is present; to assign numbers to variations in a quantifiable attribute or trait. For conditions that cannot be quantified with sufficient certainty and accuracy for the intended purposes, a description is more appropriate than measurement.

measurement-based assessment Procedures for (1) developing and selecting test items or assessment tasks by the degree to which they differentiate among examinees and for (2) administering and scoring such tests to provide statistically adequate scores for making valid generalizations regarding the psychological traits, attributes, and skills that the test items or tasks are designed to measure.

norm-referenced test A test that compares quantitative scores (such as the number of correct responses) to a normal distribution of such scores for the same age or grade. Such testing has long been used for ranking students (e.g., for allocating scarce resources) and sorting students (e.g., for forming homogeneous instructional groups).

open-ended questions Tasks that allow for various acceptable answers and for multiple approaches to an effective solution. Open-ended problems engage students in interesting situations and allow students at many levels of understanding to begin working on the problems, make their own assumptions, develop creative responses, and effectively communicate their solutions (Pandey 1991).

openness Accessibility; availability of information; receptiveness to discussion and participation; candidness; lack of secrecy.

opportunity to learn The degree to which a student has been exposed to the learning experiences needed to meet high academic standards, which is largely a function of the capacity and performance of the courses and schools the student has attended. Equitable opportunities to learn consist of equal chances for learning, with equally appropriate, favorable, or advantageous combinations of circumstances (i.e., opportunities to learn are equitable when they are responsive to the same extent to each student's needs).

outcomes Learning, results, or consequences. Equal outcomes across broad classifications of students (such as gender, race, ethnicity, etc.) that should be unrelated to performance may be evidence of equity.

performance The carrying out or bringing to completion of a physical activity or production of some significance, which displays one's knowledge and judgment while engaged in the task.

performance criterion, or standard A statement of expected performance quality that can be used to make judgments about performances that are central to the curriculum. A set of performance criteria, or standards, includes the nature of the evidence required and the quality of performance expected to demonstrate that a curriculum or content standard has been achieved. These statements often describe performances at one level, such as either adequate or exemplary, but may also describe a range of quality levels.

program evaluation The process of determining the effectiveness of an educational program in achieving its goals and, therefore, its value in comparison to its required resources.

quality Degree of excellence. The quality of assessment evidence is characterized primarily by the authenticity of the tasks, the reliability of the sample of evidence, and the credibility of the evidence for the intended purposes.

reliability The degree to which assessment evidence supports a clear, complete, and accurate understanding of the quality of an individual student's performance across time, tasks, and scorers (i.e., credibility and representativeness of the evidence).

representativeness The degree to which assessment evidence represents the valued thinking processes, knowledge, and skills that the student has developed.

rubric A set of authoritative rules to give direction to the scoring of assessment tasks or activities. To be useful, a scoring rubric must be derived from careful analysis of existing performances of varying quality. A **task-specific rubric** describes levels of performance for a particular complex performance task and guides the scoring of that task consistent with relevant performance standards. (A task-specific rubric is more specific than a performance standard and can apply a performance standard to a particular context found in a performance task.) A **general rubric** is an outline for creating task-specific rubrics, or for guiding expert judgment, where task-specific scoring rules are internal to the scorer.

scoring Discriminating among performances according to differing levels of quality and assigning a descriptive label or number to the performance. In **holistic scoring,** the entire performance as a whole is considered, and one label or number is assigned. In **analytic scoring,** separate scores are assigned to fundamentally different dimensions of the performance.

skills Abilities to perform routine mathematical procedures, typically by computational or manipulatory methods.

standard A statement about what is valued that can be used for making a judgment of quality.

standardized test A test that is administered, scored, and interpreted in a consistent manner whenever, wherever, and to whomever it is given.

standard-referenced assessment An assessment that compares the quality of performances to relevant performance criteria or standards to make a determination of the degree to which the standards have been attained or to describe progress toward the attainment of the standards.

task An authoritatively specified or assigned, purposeful, contextualized activity.

technical Relating to formal, statistical determinations of the quality of numerical scores.

test "A measuring instrument for assessing and documenting student learning. The traditional test is a single-occasion, one-dimensional, timed exercise" (Hart 1994, p. 114). "A formal, systematic procedure for obtaining a sample of [students'] behavior; the results of a test are used to make generalizations about how [students] would have performed on similar but untested behaviors" (Airasian 1991, p. 440).

understanding The ability to employ knowledge "wisely, fluently, flexibly, and aptly in particular and diverse contexts" (Wiggins 1993, p. 207).

valid Justifiable, well grounded, sound; producing the desired results, efficacious; incontestable.

valid inferences Justifiable assertions and conclusions that lead to and support desirable results. Justification is made primarily on the quality of the evidence and its adequacy for the intended purposes and their consequences.

validity The degree to which an assessment provides information that is relevant and adequate for the intended purpose. The reasonableness, quality, and efficacy of an assessment for particular educational purposes, decisions, and consequences are important issues of validity.

worthwhile mathematical tasks Tasks "that engage students' intellect; develop students' mathematical understandings and skills; stimulate students to make connections and develop a coherent framework for mathematical ideas; call for problem formulation, problem solving, and mathematical reasoning; promote communication about mathematics; represent mathematics as an ongoing human activity; display sensitivity to, and draw on, students' diverse background experiences and dispositions; promote the development of all students' dispositions to do mathematics" (NCTM 1991, p. 25).

SELECTED ASSESSMENT BIBLIOGRAPHY

The following are selected sources on assessment practices. Because of the plethora of new books and articles on this topic, a comprehensive list would be outdated before it was published. Sources cited here include both general works on the topic and those specifically on mathematics. To assist the reader, the sources below have been organized into four categories: books and book chapters, reports, journal articles, and collections of assessment tasks.

Books and Book Chapters

Airasian, Peter W. *Classroom Assessment.* New York: McGraw-Hill, 1991.

American Association for the Advancement of Science, Project 2061. *Benchmarks for Science Literacy.* Washington, D.C.: American Association for the Advancement of Science, 1993.

Berlak, Harold, Fred M. Newmann, Elizabeth Adams, Douglas A. Archbald, Tyrrell Burgess, John Raven, and Thomas A. Romberg. *Toward a New Science of Educational Testing and Assessment.* Albany, N.Y.: State University of New York Press, 1992.

Brandt, Ronald S. *Readings from Educational Leadership: Performance Assessment.* Alexandria, Va.: Association for Supervision and Curriculum Development, 1992.

Bright, George, A. Edward Uprichard, and Janice Jetton. *Mathematics Program: A Guide to Evaluation.* Newbury Park, Calif.: Corwin Press, 1993.

Charles, Randall I., and Edward A. Silver, eds. *Research Agenda for Mathematics Education: The Teaching and Assessing of Mathematical Problem Solving.* Hillsdale, N.J.: Lawrence Erlbaum Associates, 1988.

Fredericksen, Norman, Robert J. Mislevy, and Isaac I. Bejar, eds. *Test Theory for a New Generation of Tests.* Hillsdale, N.J.: Lawrence Erlbaum Associates, 1993.

Hart, Diane. *Authentic Assessment: A Handbook for Educators.* Menlo Park, Calif.: Addison-Wesley, 1994.

Kallik, Bera, and Ross Brewer, eds. *Exemplars: A Teacher's Solution.* Underhill, Vt.: Exemplars, 1993.

Kamii, Constance, ed. *Achievement Testing in the Early Grades.* Washington, D.C.: National Association of Education for Young Children, 1990.

Kulm, Gerald. *Assessing Higher Order Thinking in Mathematics.* Washington, D.C.: American Association for the Advancement of Science, 1990.

————. *Mathematics Assessment: What Works in the Classroom.* San Francisco: Jossey-Bass, 1994.

Leder, Gilah, ed. *Assessment and Learning of Mathematics.* Hawthorn, Victoria [Australia]: Australian Council for Educational Research, 1992.

Lesh, Richard, and Susan J. Lamon, eds. *Assessment of Authentic Performance in School Mathematics.* Washington, D.C.: American Association for the Advancement of Science, 1992.

Mathematical Sciences Education Board, National Research Council. *Measuring What Counts: A Conceptual Guide for Mathematics Assessment.* Washington, D.C.: National Academy Press, 1993.

Messick, Samuel. "Validity." In *Educational Measurement,* edited by Robert L. Linn, 3rd ed., pp.13–103. New York: American Council on Education and Macmillan, 1989.

Mitchell, Ruth. *Testing for Learning: How New Approaches to Evaluation Can Improve American Schools.* New York: Free Press, 1992.

Niss, Mogens, ed. *Cases of Assessment in Mathematics Education—an ICMI Study.* Dordrecht, Netherlands: Kluwer Academic Publishers, 1993.

————. *Investigations into Assessment in Mathematics Education—an ICMI Study.* Dordrecht, Netherlands: Kluwer Academic Publishers, 1993.

Northwest Regional Educational Laboratory. *Innovative Assessment: Science and Mathematics Bibliographies.* Washington, D.C.: U.S. Department of Education, 1993.

Office of Technology Assessment. *Testing in American Schools: Asking the Right Questions.* Washington, D.C.: Office of Technology Assessment, 1992.

Perrone, Vito, ed. *Expanding Student Assessment.* Alexandria, Va.: Association for Supervision and Curriculum Development, 1991.

Popham, W. James. *Classroom Assessment: What Teachers Need to Know.* Boston: Allyn & Bacon, 1995.

Regional Educational Laboratory Network Program on Science and Mathematics Alternative Assessment. *Improving Science and Mathematics Education: A Database and Catalog of Alternative Assessments.* Portland, Oreg.: Northwest Regional Educational Laboratory, 1994.

Resnick, Lauren B., and Daniel P. Resnick. "Assessing the Thinking Curriculum: New Tools for Educational Reform." In *Changing Assessments: Alternative Views of Aptitude, Achievement, and Instruction,* edited by Bernard R. Gifford and Mary C. O'Connor, pp. 37–75. Boston: Kluwer Academic Publishers, 1992.

Romberg, Thomas A., ed. *Mathematics Assessment and Evaluation: Imperatives for Mathematics Educators.* Albany, N.Y.: State University of New York Press, 1992.

————. *Reform in School Mathematics and Authentic Assessment.* Albany, N.Y.: State University of New York Press, 1995.

Silver, Edward, Jeremy Kilpatrick, and Beth Schlesinger. *Thinking through Mathematics.* New York: College Entrance Examination Board, 1990.

Snow, Richard E., and David F. Lohman. "Implications of Cognitive Psychology for Educational Measurement." In *Educational Measurement,* edited by Robert L. Linn, 3rd ed., pp. 263–331. New York: American Council on Education and Macmillan, 1989.

Stiggins, Richard J. *Student-Centered Classroom Assessment.* New York: Merrill Publishing Co., 1994.

Stiggins, Richard J., and Nancy F. Conklin. *In Teachers' Hands—Investigating the Practices of Classroom Assessment.* Albany, N.Y.: State University of New York Press, 1992.

Webb, Norman L. "Assessment of Students' Knowledge of Mathematics: Steps toward a Theory." In *Handbook of Research on Mathematics and Learning,* edited by Douglas A. Grouws, pp. 661–86. New York: Macmillan, 1992.

————, ed. *Assessment in the Mathematics Classroom: 1993 Yearbook.* Reston, Va.: National Council of Teachers of Mathematics, 1993.

Wiggins, Grant P. *Assessing Student Performance: Exploring the Purpose and Limits of Testing.* San Francisco: Jossey-Bass, 1993.

Wittrock, Merlin C., and Eva L. Baker, eds. *Testing and Cognition.* Englewood Cliffs, N.J.: Prentice Hall, 1991.

Reports

American Association of School Administrators. *The Changing Face of Testing and Assessment: Problems and Solutions.* Arlington, Va.: American Association of School Administrators, 1991.

Archbald, Douglas A., and Fred M. Newmann. *Beyond Standardized Testing: Assessing Authentic Academic Achievement in the Secondary School.* Reston, Va.: National Association of Secondary School Principals, 1988.

Baker, Eva L., Pamela R. Aschbacher, David Niemi, and Edynn Sato. *CRESST Performance Assessment Models: Assessing Content Area Explanations.* Los Angeles: National Center for Research on Evaluation, Standards, and Student Testing, 1992.

Baron, Joan B., ed. *Assessment as an Opportunity to Learn.* Hartford, Conn.: Connecticut State Department of Education, 1993.

Estrin, Elise T. *Alternative Assessment: Issues in Language, Culture, and Equity.* San Francisco: Far West Laboratory, 1993.

Grace, Cathy, and Elizabeth F. Shores. *The Portfolio and Its Use: Developmentally Appropriate Assessment of Young Children.* Little Rock, Ark.: Southern Association on Children Under Six, 1991.

Madaus, George F., Mary M. West, Maryellen Harmon, Richard G. Lomax, and Katherine A. Viator. *The Influence of Testing on Teaching Math and Science in Grades 4–12.* Chestnut Hill, Mass.: Center for the Study of Testing, Evaluation, and Educational Policy, 1992.

Mathematical Sciences Education Board, National Research Council. *For Good Measure: Principles and Goals for Mathematics Assessment.* Washington, D.C.: National Academy Press, 1991.

McTighe, Jay, and Steven Ferrara. *Assessing Learning in the Classroom.* Washington, D.C.: National Education Association, 1994.

National Center on Educational Outcomes. *Testing Accommodations for Students with Disabilities: A Review of the Literature.* Washington, D.C.: National Center on Educational Outcomes, n.d.

National Council on Education Standards and Testing. *Raising Standards for American Education.* Washington, D.C.: National Council on Education Standards and Testing, 1992.

National Education Association. *The Role of High-Stakes Testing in School Reform.* Report to the National Education Goals Panel. Washington, D.C.: National Education Association, 1993.

National Education Goals Panel. *Promises to Keep: Creating High Standards for American Students.* Washington, D.C.: National Education Goals Panel, 1993.

Petit, Marge. *Getting Started: Vermont Mathematics Portfolio—Learning How to Show Your Best!* Cabot, Vt.: Cabot School, 1992.

Simmons, Walter, and Lauren Resnick. *Assessment as the Catalyst of School Reform.* Pittsburgh, Pa.: Learning Research and Development Center, 1993.

Vermont Department of Education. *Looking beyond "The Answer."* Montpelier, Vt.: Vermont Department of Education, 1991.

White, Sheida. *Overview of NAEP Assessment Frameworks.* Washington, D.C.: U.S. Department of Education, 1994.

Winfield, Linda F., and Michael D. Woodard. *Assessment, Equity, and Diversity in Reforming America's Schools.* CSE Technical Report 372. Los Angeles: National Center for Research on Evaluation, Standards, and Student Testing, 1994.

Journal Articles

American Federation of Teachers, National Council on Measurement in Education, National Education Association. "Standards for Teacher Competence in Educational Assessment of Students." *Educational Measurement: Issues and Practice* 9 (4) (1990): 30–32.

Arter, Judith A., and Vicki Spandel. "Using Portfolios of Student Work in Instruction and Assessment (an NCME Instructional Module)." *Educational Measurement: Issues and Practice* 11 (1) (1992): 36–44.

"Assessing Mathematics." Special issue of *Educational Studies in Mathematics* 27 (December 1994).

Baxter, Gail P., Richard J. Shavelson, Sally J. Herman, Katherine A. Brown, and James R. Valadez. "Mathematics Performance Assessment: Technical Quality and Diverse Student Impact." *Journal for Research in Mathematics Education* 24 (May 1993): 190–216.

Burger, Susan E., and Donald L. Burger. "Determining the Validity of Performance-Based Assessment." *Educational Measurement: Issues and Practice* 13 (1) (1994): 9–15.

Cain, Ralph W., and Patricia A. Kenney. "A Joint Vision for Classroom Assessment." *Mathematics Teacher* 85 (November 1992): 612–15.

Cobb, Paul. "Assessment of a Problem-Centered Second-Grade Mathematics Project." *Journal for Research in Mathematics Education* 22 (January 1991): 3–29.

Feuer, Michael J., and Kathleen Fulton. "Educational Testing Abroad and Lessons for the United States." *Educational Measurement: Issues and Practice* 13 (2) (1994): 31–39.

Gearhart, Maryl, and Joan L. Herman. "Portfolio Assessment: Whose Work Is It? (Issues in the Use of Classroom Assignments for Accountability)." *Evaluation Comment* (Winter 1995): 1–16.

Glaser, Robert. "Instructional Technology and the Measurement of Learning Outcomes: Some Questions." *Educational Measurement: Issues and Practice* 13 (4) (1994): 6–8.

————. "Criterion-Referenced Tests: Part I. Origins." *Educational Measurement: Issues and Practice* 13 (4) (1994): 9–11.

————. "Criterion-Referenced Tests: Part II. Unfinished Business." *Educational Measurement: Issues and Practice* 13 (4) (1994): 27–30.

Hambleton, Ronald K. "The Rise and Fall of Criterion-Referenced Measurement?" *Educational Measurement: Issues and Practice* 13 (4) (1994): 21–26.

Hambleton, Ronald K., and Edward Murphy. "A Psychometric Perspective on Authentic Measurement." *Applied Measurement in Education* 5 (1) (1992): 1–16.

Herman, Janice L. "What Research Tells Us about Good Assessment." *Educational Leadership* 49 (8) (1992): 74–78.

Hughes, Selma. "What Is Alternative/Authentic Assessment and How Does It Impact Special Education?" *Educational Horizons* 72 (7) (1993): 28–35.

Johnston, Peter H. "Constructive Evaluation and the Improvement of Teaching and Learning." *Teachers College Record* 90 (4) (1989): 509–28.

Kane, Michael. "Validating the Performance Standards Associated with Passing Scores." *Review of Educational Research* 62 (3) (1994): 425–61.

Knight, Pam. "How I Use Portfolios in Mathematics." *Educational Leadership* 49 (8) (1992): 71–72.

Koretz, Daniel, Brian Stecher, Stephen Klein, and Daniel McCaffrey. "The Vermont Portfolio Assessment Program: Findings and Implications." *Educational Measurement: Issues and Practice* 13 (3) (1994): 5–16.

Lajoie, Susanne P., and Alan M. Lesgold. "Dynamic Assessment of Proficiency for Solving Procedural Knowledge Tasks." *Educational Psychologist* 27 (3) (1992): 365–84.

Lester, Frank K., and Diana L. Kroll. "Evaluation: A New Vision." *Mathematics Teacher* 84 (April 1991): 276–83.

Linn, Robert. "Criterion-Referenced Measurement: A Valuable Perspective Clouded by Surplus Meaning." *Educational Measurement: Issues and Practice* 13 (4) (1994): 12–14.

Linn, Robert L., Eva L. Baker, and Stephen B. Dunbar. "Complex, Performance-Based Assessment: Expectations and Validation Criteria." *Educational Researcher* 2 (8) (1991): 15–21.

Linn, Robert L., and Elizabeth Burton. "Performance-Based Assessment: Implications of Task Specificity." *Educational Measurement: Issues and Practice.* 13 (7) (1994): 5–8.

Messick, Samuel. "The Interplay of Evidence and Consequences in the Validation of Performance Assessments." *Educational Researcher* 23 (2) (1994): 13–23.

Millman, Jason. "Criterion-Referenced Testing 30 Years Later: Promise Broken, Promise Kept." *Educational Measurement: Issues and Practice* 13 (4) (Winter 1994): 19–20.

Moss, Pamela A. "Can There Be Validity without Reliability?" *Educational Researcher* 23 (2) (1994): 5–12.

Moss, Pamela A., Jamie S. Beck, Catherine Ebbs, Barbara Matson, James Muchmore, Dorothy Steele, and Caroline Taylor. "Portfolios, Accountability, and an Interpretive Approach to Validity." *Educational Measurement: Issues and Practice* 11 (3) (1992): 12–21.

Pickering, James W., and Jeanne C. Bowers. "In the Field: Assessing Value-Added Outcomes Assessment." *Measurement and Evaluation in Counseling and Development* 20 (1) (1990): 215–21.

Popham, James W. "The Instructional Consequences of Criterion-Referenced Clarity." *Educational Measurement: Issues and Practice* 13 (4) (Winter 1994): 15–18.

Quellmalz, Edys S. "Developing Criteria for Performance Assessments: The Missing Link." *Applied Measurement in Education* 4 (4) (1991): 319–31.

Rudner, Lawrence M., and Carol Boston. "Performance Assessment." *ERIC Review* 3 (1) (1993): 2–12.

Sammons, Kay B., Beth Kobett, Joan Heiss, and Francis Fennell. "Linking Instruction and Assessment in the Mathematics Classroom." *Arithmetic Teacher* 39 (February 1992): 11–16.

Schafer, William D. "Essential Assessment Skills in Professional Education of Teachers." *Educational Measurement: Issues and Practice* 10 (1) (1991): 3–6.

Shafroth, Chantal. "A Comparison of University Entrance Examinations in the United States and in Europe." *Focus* 13 (3) (1993): 1, 11–14.

Shavelson, Richard J., Gail P. Baxter, and Jerry Pine. "Performance Assessments: Political Rhetoric Measurement Reality." *Educational Researcher* 21 (4) (1992): 22–27.

Smith, Mary Lee, and Claire Rottenberg. "Unintended Consequences of External Testing in Elementary Schools." *Educational Measurement: Issues and Practice* 10 (4) (1991): 7–11.

Spangler, Denise A. "Assessing Students' Beliefs about Mathematics." *Arithmetic Teacher* (November 1992): 148–52.

Stake, Robert E. "The Teacher, Standardized Testing, and Prospects of Revolution." *Phi Delta Kappan* 73 (3) (1991): 243–47.

Stiggins, Richard J. "Facing the Challenges of a New Era of Educational Assessment." *Applied Measurement in Education* 4 (4) (1991): 263–371.

————. "Relevant Classroom Assessment Training for Teachers." *Educational Measurement: Issues and Practice* 10 (1) (1991): 7–12.

Stiggins, Richard J., David A. Frisbie, and Philip A. Griswold. "Inside High School Grading Practices: Building a Research Agenda." *Educational Measurement: Issues and Practice* 8 (2) (1989): 5–14.

Szetela, Walter, and Cynthia Nicol. "Evaluating Problem Solving in Mathematics." *Educational Leadership* 49 (8) (1992): 42–45.

Taylor, Catherine. "Assessment for Measurement or Standards: The Peril and Promise of Large-Scale Assessment Reform." *American Educational Research Journal* 31 (2) (1994): 231–62.

Thompson, Alba G., and Diane J. Briars. "Implementing the Standards: Assessing Students' Learning to Inform Teaching: The Message in NCTM's Evaluation Standards." *Arithmetic Teacher* 37 (December 1989): 22–26.

Collections of Assessment Tasks

Binns, Barbara, Hugh Burkhardt, John Gillespie, Steve Maddern, and Malcolm Swan. *Balanced Assessment in Mathematics: An Illustrated Introduction.* Nottingham, England: Shell Centre for Mathematical Education, 1987.

Burns, Marilyn. *Writing in the Math Class, Grades 3 through 8.* Sausalito, Calif.: Marilyn Burns Education Associates, forthcoming.

Clark, Clare, and Betsy Carter. *Math in Stride: Student Activities for Performance Assessment, Grades 3, 4, 5, and 6.* Menlo Park, Calif.: Addison-Wesley, 1994.

Clarke, David. *Assessment Alternatives in Mathematics.* Carlton, Victoria [Australia]: Curriculum Corporation, 1989.

Educational Testing Service. *Performance Assessment Sampler: A Workbook.* Princeton, N.J.: Educational Testing Service, 1993.

Mathematical Sciences Education Board, National Research Council. *Measuring Up: Prototypes for Mathematics Assessment.* Washington, D.C.: National Academy Press, 1993.

Mathematics Centre. *Practical Suggestions for Developing and Assessing Mathematics Coursework—Part One and Part Two.* W. Berks, England: Foulsham & Co., 1989.

Mumme, Judy. *Portfolio Assessment in Mathematics.* Santa Barbara, Calif.: California Mathematics Project, 1991.

National Center for Restructuring Education, Schools, and Teaching. *Authentic Assessment in Practice: A Collection of Portfolios, Performance Tasks, Exhibitions, and Documentation.* New York: National Center for Restructuring Education, Schools, and Teaching, 1993.

Northwest Regional Educational Laboratory. *Assessing Mathematical Power.* Videotape and trainer's guide. Portland, Oreg.: Northwest Regional Educational Laboratory, 1992.

Pandey, Tej. *A Sampler of Mathematics Assessment.* California Assessment Program. Sacramento, Calif.: California Department of Education, 1991.

Stenmark, Jean K. *Assessment Alternatives in Mathematics: An Overview of Assessment Techniques That Promote Learning.* Berkeley, Calif.: EQUALS, University of California, 1989.

————, ed. *Mathematics Assessment: Myths, Models, Good Questions, and Practical Suggestions.* Reston, Va.: National Council of Teachers of Mathematics, 1991.

Sutton, John T., Robert J. Marzano, John S. Kendall, and Stephen J. Bloom. *Mathematical Tasks and the NCTM "Curriculum and Evaluation Standards."* Aurora, Colo.: Mid-Continent Regional Educational Laboratory, 1992.

Vaille, John, and Harold Kushins. *Creative Math Assessment.* Watertown, Mass.: Tom Snyder Productions, 1993.

Westley, Joan. *Puddle Questions: Assessing Mathematical Thinking (Grades 1, 2, 3, 4, 5, 6).* Palo Alto, Calif.: Creative Publications, 1994.

Wu, Ling-Erl Eileen T., ed. *Japanese University Entrance Examination Problems in Mathematics.* Washington, D.C.: Mathematical Association of America, 1993.

REFERENCES

Airasian, Peter W. *Classroom Assessment.* New York: McGraw-Hill, 1991.

Blume, Glendon W., and Robert F. Nicely, Jr. *A Guide for Reviewing School Mathematics Programs.* Reston, Va.: National Council of Teachers of Mathematics; Alexandria, Va.: Association for Supervision and Curriculum Development, 1991.

Carpenter, Thomas P., and Elizabeth Fennema. "Cognitively Guided Instruction: Building on the Knowledge of Students and Teachers." In "Reform of School Mathematics in the United States," special issue edited by Walter G. Secada. *International Journal of Educational Research* 17 (1992): 457–70.

Clarke, David J. *Assessment Alternatives in Mathematics.* Carlton, Victoria [Australia]: Curriculum Corporation, 1989.

Connecticut State Department of Education. "Performance Task Sampler." Document produced as part of the Connecticut Common Core of Learning Assessment Project. Hartford, Conn.: Connecticut State Department of Education, 1991.

Darling-Hammond, Linda. "Performance-Based Assessment and Educational Equity." *Harvard Educational Review* 64 (1994): 5–30.

Gerberich, J. Raymond, Harry A. Green, and Albert N. Jorgensen. *Measurement and Evaluation in the Modern School.* New York: David McKay, 1962.

Hart, Diane. *Authentic Assessment: A Handbook for Educators.* Menlo Park, Calif.: Addison-Wesley, 1994.

Lajoie, Susanne P. "Technologies for Extending Statistical Learning." In *Handbook on Assessment in Statistics Education,* edited by Iddo Gal and Joan Garfield. Unpublished manuscript, n.d.

Lajoie, Susanne P., Nancy C. Lavigne, Steven Muncie, and Tara V. Wilkie. "Monitoring Student Progress in Statistical Comprehension and Skill." In *Reflections on Statistics: Agendas for Learning, Teaching, and Assessment in K–12,* edited by Susanne Lajoie. Hillsdale, N.J.: Erlbaum Associates, forthcoming.

Lavigne, Nancy C. "Authentic Assessment: A Library of Exemplars for Enhancing Statistics Performance." Master's thesis, McGill University, 1994.

Lesh, Richard A., and Susan J. Lamon. "Trends, Goals, and Priorities in Mathematics Assessment." In *Assessment of Authentic Performance in School Mathematics,* edited by Richard A. Lesh and Susan J. Lamon, pp. 3–16. Washington, D.C.: American Association for the Advancement of Science, 1992.

————. "Assessing Authentic Mathematical Performance." In *Assessment of Authentic Performance in School Mathematics,* edited by Richard A. Lesh and Susan J. Lamon, pp.17–62. Washington, D.C.: American Association for the Advancement of Science, 1992.

Madaus, George F. "A Technological and Historical Consideration of Equity Issues Associated with Proposals to Change the Nation's Testing Policy." *Harvard Educational Review* 64 (1994): 76–95.

Marolda, Maria R., and Patricia S. Davidson. "Assessing Mathematical Abilities and Learning Approaches." In *Windows of Opportunity: Mathematics for Students with Special Needs,* edited by Carol A. Thornton and Nancy S. Bley, pp. 83–113. Reston, Va.: National Council of Teachers of Mathematics, 1994.

Mathematical Sciences Education Board, National Research Council. *Everybody Counts: A Report to the Nation on the Future of Mathematics Education.* Washington, D.C.: National Academy Press, 1989.

————— . *Measuring What Counts: A Conceptual Guide for Mathematics Assessment.* Washington, D.C.: National Academy Press, 1993.

Meisels, Samuel J., Margo Dichtelmiller, Aviva Dorfman, Judy R. Jablon, and Dorothea B. Marsden. *The Work Sampling System Resource Guide.* Ann Arbor, Mich.: Rebus Planning Associates, 1993.

National Council of Teachers of Mathematics. *Curriculum and Evaluation Standards for School Mathematics.* Reston, Va.: National Council of Teachers of Mathematics, 1989.

————— . *Professional Standards for Teaching Mathematics.* Reston, Va.: National Council of Teachers of Mathematics, 1991.

Pandey, Tej. *A Sampler of Mathematics Assessment.* California Assessment Program. Sacramento, Calif.: California Department of Education, 1991.

Petit, Marge. "Getting Started: Vermont Mathematics Portfolio—Learning How to Show Your Best!" Cabot, Vt.: Cabot School, 1992.

Shafroth, Chantal. "A Comparison of University Entrance Examinations in the United States and in Europe." *Focus* 13 (3) (1993): 1, 11–14.

Stephens, Max, and Barry McCrae. "Assessing Problem Solving in a School System: Principles to Practice." *Australian Senior Mathematics Journal* [Australian Association of Mathematics Teachers, Adelaide, South Australia], in press.

Victorian Board of Studies. *Specialist Mathematics Units 3 and 4, Common Assessment Task 1.* Carlton, Victoria [Australia]: Victorian Board of Studies, 1994.

————— . *VCE Study Design: Mathematics.* Carlton, Victoria [Australia]: Victorian Board of Studies, 1994.

Wiggins, Grant P. *Assessing Student Performance: Exploring the Purpose and Limits of Testing.* San Francisco: Jossey-Bass, 1993.

Wu, Ling-Erl Eileen T., ed. *Japanese University Entrance Examination Problems in Mathematics.* Washington, D.C.: Mathematical Association of America, 1993.

Please remember that this is a library book,
and that it belongs only temporarily to each
person who uses it. Be considerate. Do
not write in this, or any, library book.